Why We Loved To Fly, And How It Showed

A Collection of Airline Memories
By Captain Ron Stowe

Published by:
LAD Custom Publishing
Buford, Georgia

Dedication

This book is dedicated to my wife Carol. Without her love, encouragement, faith, and devotion, my hopes, and dreams might never have become reality. She is the wind beneath my wings.

Table of Contents

Chapter 1
Huff-Daland Dusters

Cotton was "King" in the plantation economy of the slavery states in the Deep South, but this was not simply a Southern phenomenon. Cotton was one of the world's first luxury commodities, after sugar and tobacco. It was the leading American export from 1803 to 1937.

The Dreaded Boll Weevil

Beginning in the late 19th century, the boll weevil migrated into the United States from Mexico. The small beetle, which feeds on cotton buds and flowers, infested all U.S. cotton-growing areas, devastating the industry and the people working in the American South.

In the early 1920s, agricultural and aviation researchers came together to find a solution to the boll weevil infestation that was destroying cotton crops. A team at the U.S. Department of Agriculture's field laboratory in Tallulah, Louisiana, along with Army pilots and aircraft, developed improvements that determined "dusting" of insecticide powder from the air would be the most effective form of treatment.

The Amazing Miss Fitz

Catherine FitzGerald, daughter of John F. FitzGerald and Catherine Ready FitzGerald, was born September 21, 1897 in Ogdensburg, New York. She was educated at St. Mary's Academy and the Ogdensburg Business School before being hired by the Huff-Daland Company as a stenographer in 1923. Formed by Thomas Huff and Elliot Daland, the company produced a series of biplanes as trainers, observation planes, and light bombers for the U.S. Army and Navy. From 1923-1924, Huff-Daland developed the first aircraft designed for crop dusting. In 1927, the corporation became the Huff-Daland Division of the Keystone Aircraft Corporation.

After the company relocated its headquarters to Bristol, Pennsylvania in 1925, Catherine chose to remain close to her home in New York. However, in 1926, she changed her mind and moved to Monroe, Louisiana, to work for Huff- Daland Dusters, a subsidiary of the Huff-Daland Company. She was destined to become the first woman ever to be elected to the board of directors of an American airline.

The Puffer

The Huff-Daland Manufacturing Company modified its sturdy Petrel military biplane with a large hopper for chemicals and spraying equipment and established the nation's first aerial dusting business, Huff-Daland Duster Company of Macon, Georgia in 1924. The aircraft was nicknamed the "Puffer". It was headquartered in Macon, Georgia, because of the city offering an adequate airfield to base the operation. Spraying was extensively conducted over Georgia peach orchards, pecan orchards, and cotton fields in neighboring states.

In 1925, Huff-Daland Dusters moved to Monroe, Louisiana, where influential businessmen were enthusiastic about aviation and agreed to provide an airfield with a hanger 160 feet long and 60 feet wide.

The company consented to occupy the airfield for three years and agreed to make Monroe headquarters for all its operations. C.E. Woolman was hired by Huff-Daland Dusters as an entomologist because he was familiar with local conditions, knew most of the planters, and was able to negotiate dusting contracts.

Mr. C. E. Woolman left his position with Louisiana State University's Agricultural Extension Department and in the off-season traveled with the company to Peru, where they helped to establish crop-dusting and passenger services. With this experience, Woolman returned to the United States and in 1928, he led a group of local investors to acquire Huff- Daland Dusters assets.

Delta Air Service

In the summer of 1928, the managerial staff of the Huff-Daland dusting operation consisted of Captain Harold R. Harris, a well-known army pilot and C. E. Woolman, both were vice-presidents. Irwin E. Auerbach was the controller, and Catherine FitzGerald was secretary. In July, as a show of regard for the employees, the three men were given 330 shares of Huff-Daland common stock, and FitzGerald received 10 shares.

The group had developed a contingency plan to purchase the assets of the dusting operation if the opportunity ever arose. In August of 1928, it appeared that an opportunity had arisen. Over the next few months, numerous attempts to put together a deal failed to produce any results.

Then on November 12th, Mr. Woolman signed an agreement with Keystone – Huff-Daland, in which he, acting for himself and his associates, would purchase the dusting operations assets for $20,000 in cash and $20,000 in notes. On November 18th,   C.E. Woolman, Travis Oliver, a prominent Monroe banker, and D.Y. Smith, a wealthy local planter, appeared before a notary republic in Monroe to begin the process of incorporating a new company, Delta Air Service Inc, whose name had been suggested by Catherine FitzGerald after the lush Mississippi Delta region in which the enterprise was based.

The company received it charter on December 3rd. Initially the board consisted of Smith as president, Woolman as first vice-president, Harris as second-vice president, and Oliver as treasurer.

A new prospect presented itself in late 1928. Delta Air Service won a contract, awarded by the Army Corps of Engineers, to fly up and down the Mississippi River inspecting the levee system during the flood season. The aircraft used to inspect "Old Man River" was an open cockpit Travel Air with pontoons. Before long, Woolman began to plan a significant new type of operation. His thoughts centered on creating a passenger carrier.

An Airline is Born
In 1929, Woolman purchased the assets of Fox Flying Services, which included an open-cockpit biplane, used for taking people on joyrides, and another plane: a high-wing, single-engine, six-place, enclosed-cabin Travel Air

S-6000B. Woolman had his airliner, plus an option on another Travel Air. In return, Fox received $20,000 in shares of Delta stock and could purchase an additional $35,000 worth of shares, making him the largest Delta stockholder by far.

On June 17, 1929, John Howe, a Delta employee, was at the controls of the Travel Air that took off for the company's first passenger flight from Dallas, Texas, to Jackson, Mississippi, with stops in Shreveport and Monroe, Louisiana. By June 1930, Delta's route had expanded eastward to Atlanta, the fastest-growing city in the South, and westward to Fort Worth, Texas. This service was terminated in October 1930 after the Post Office awarded the airmail route to an American Airlines predecessor. Delta's lack of success in winning a commercial airmail contract—the bread and butter of any aspiring airline—jeopardized its existence. Delta Air Service suspended passenger service and sold its assets to its competitor.

In 1930, the name of the company was changed to Delta Air Corporation. Mr. Woolman informed the press that the same management staff would lead Delta under the new corporate form and name. Smith would continue as president, Woolman as vice-president, and Oliver as treasurer. Oliver's former duties as secretary were assigned to Catherine FitzGerald. The board of directors was to be composed of these four plus Malcolm S. Biedenharn, the first man in the United States to bottle Coca-Cola, and Prentiss Atkins, an original investor in Delta and an aviation enthusiast.

The ever capable and devotedly loyal secretary, Catherine FitzGerald, had not wanted to move south from her native Ogdensburg, New York, but finally come to enjoy living in the region. From the beginning, her role went beyond that of typing letters and keeping track of records. As one of the company's' officers and directors, she was consulted on policy matters as well. Miss Fitz had influenced her superiors not to permit the wives of dusting personnel to accompany their husbands on trips away from Monroe to other agricultural locations, apparently because she thought that the men would be distracted from their work.

Airmail Route 24

In 1934, Delta was competing for an airmail route from Fort Worth, TX to Charleston, SC. The company would need to raise additional funds and borrow money to finance the airline operations. At the request of Travis Oliver, the board passed resolutions authorizing an increase in stock from 5,000 to 8,000 shares at five dollars per share, contingent upon the company's obtaining the contract for route 24. Two thousand shares were set aside for Joseph H. Biedenharn and Carl H. McHenry for agreeing to guarantee the note. In June, Biedenharn announced that Delta had been selected to carry the mail on route 24.

Shortly thereafter Catherine FitzGerald resigned as secretary and member of the board. She was asked to step down to make way for McHenry, who took over both roles. Like the devoted company servant that she was, Catharine loyally complied. Obviously not a militant feminist, she seems to have been contented with her subsequent appointment as assistant treasurer and her duties as Woolman's private secretary. Over the years FitzGerald would become an institution in herself and remained in active service with the company until after Woolman's death.

The Move to Atlanta

Increasingly, it had become apparent that Atlanta was more strategically located in the future of commercial aviation in the South. In 1940, the city of Atlanta and Delta had signed an agreement whereby the city agreed to contribute $50,000 for construction of a new hanger and office building for Delta if it would move its headquarters to Atlanta. In turn, Delta agreed to pay the remaining construction costs and then assume a 20-year lease for the new facilities. On Jan. 16, 1941, Delta had secured a $500,000 loan from Atlanta's Trust Company of Georgia, thus allowing it to make a public announcement of the move. Construction of the hanger and office building was completed in early 1941, and Delta moved into its new facilities on March 1st.

Miss Fitz accompanied Woolman, her boss from Monroe, to set up headquarters in Atlanta. She rented a small three-room apartment on East Walker Avenue, near the airport, in College Park. She changed apartments a couple of times, but she remained living in College Park garage apartments throughout her long career with Delta.

Delta's network was an unbranched string of twelve cities from Fort Worth to Charleston, SC. That December it scheduled ten departures a day at Atlanta: three to Ft Worth, one to Birmingham and two each to Cincinnati, Charleston, and Savannah. Those ten flights were Delta's whole schedule.

By the summer of 1945, Delta was in an excellent position for future growth. The name of the company was changed to Delta Air Lines. Although Delta Air Lines kept a crop-dusting division until 1966, by 1938 expanding airmail and passenger service operations begin earning more than crop-dusting profits. Catherine FitzGerald was sitting in her office at 3:30 pm when the telephone rang. Delta, in contest among twelve other airlines, had been awarded the longest single new route ever granted by the CAB – a 1028 mile run from Chicago to Miami. As she listened to the voice on the other end of the call, her eyes widened as she tried taking shorthand notes while gasping, laughing, and trying to say six things at once. Within moments, the halls of the Delta headquarters were filled with excited employees yelling, Chicago to Miami! Chicago clear to Miami!

Post War Expansion

By 1947, the airline operated 44 daily flights between 35 cities in thirteen states, and employed 2,050 people, with 1,000 of them in Atlanta. Delta's headquarters more than doubled in size with a $1 million addition of a two-story executive office building and a second maintenance hangar. The office space in these original buildings are still used for company business by staff and executives, and houses the office of Delta CEO, Ed

Bastian, who still uses the desk that was purchased for Delta's founder C.E. Woolman.

Emerging from a painful period of postwar readjustment, Delta was celebrating its twentieth anniversary as a passenger carrier on June 1, 1949. At a banquet climaxing a spring sales meeting in Atlanta, Catherine FitzGerald, Secretary to the President and Assistant Treasurer, cut a three-tiered birthday cake at a head table graced by a model of the 1929 Travel Air, while C.E. Woolman and other Delta offices looked on. The ceremony was broadcast on the WCON radio station during their 6:30 news program.

Mr. Woolman frequently walked down to the hanger to talk to some of his employees. He knew most of them by name and would often ask about their family members, calling them by name. One of his famous quotes was, "No one person is an airline. An airline is a team. It must be friendly, courteous, cooperative, efficient and bound as closely as a devoted family." Delta truly was a family of dedicated employees that genuinely cared for each other. His hobby was growing orchids. During the graduation ceremony each new stewardess had one of the prized orchids pinned to her lapel by Mr. Woolman.

Early in 1966, Catherine FitzGerald was honored on her fortieth anniversary with Delta and its dusting predecessor. Mr. Woolman affixed to her lapel a jeweled Delta pin symbolizing the anniversary along with one of his rare orchids. Her long-time boss, said "Miss Fitz, as she was known around the Delta corporate office, was little more than a "schoolgirl" with a talent for running columns of figures in her head, when she started her career in aviation". She was the longest serving Delta employee at the time.

The End of an Era

In September of 1966, Mr. Woolman was scheduled for surgery in Houston to correct a threatening aneurysm. Only a handful of company executives and Catherine FitzGerald knew the real purpose of the trip. Everyone else was told that he would be attending a meeting of aviation personalities in Wyoming and doing some fishing. The operation was completed on September 7th and appeared to be a success. Then suddenly, on September 11th, Mr. Woolman died.

Two antique survivors from the Huff-Daland's original fleet of crop-dusting planes were crated up and shipped to Atlanta in moving vans in November of 1966. Led by mechanic Gene Barry, who began his relationship with Delta in the early 1930s, one of the airplanes was stripped to its basic components and a complete restoration was completed. Six months later, the finished project was rolled out for public admiration prior to being shipped to the Smithsonian Institution as a permanent memorial to Mr. Woolman.

On January 18, 1968, a completely restored Huff-Daland Duster officially was presented to the Smithsonian Institution in memory of its departed founder, C.E. Woolman, after a brief statement of presentation by Catherine FitzGerald. In the audience was Woolman's daughters and grandchildren.

After retiring in 1968, Catherine continued to live in her garage apartment until 1983, when a hip injury forced her to move into a nursing home. In 1986, because of failing health and mental deterioration, a court appointed guardian took charge of her business affairs.

When she died of heart failure at the South Fulton Hospital on September 13, 1987, at age 89, most people were shocked to learn that she had amassed a stock portfolio, which included shares in Exxon Corp., Phillips Petroleum Co., General Dynamics Corp., General Electric Co., and 126,744 shares of Delta Air Lines stock with a value of over $5 million dollars. She still owned a 1969 Chevy Bel Air with 23,000 miles on the odometer.

Miss FitzGerald never married and had no children. She left no heirs. The bulk of her estate was distributed to 11 Catholic church organizations in Georgia and New York.

Described as a devoutly religious woman, Catherine FitzGerald attended the St. John the Evangelist Church in Hapeville. Her funeral service was held at the church. Kenneth Brown, a Fairburn lawyer and long-time friend, who handled her will said, "She never told me why she chose not to spend more of her money. The people who knew her respected her privacy. She led her life the way she wanted." Perry Hunter, a neighbor for 37 years, who drove Miss FitzGerald to 5 o'clock mass said, "A few of us neighbors knew she was wealthy, but never asked why she didn't move to a nicer place." During an interview in 1984 in the Atlanta Constitution newspaper, a reporter asked why she never married – perhaps to one of the pilots. She laughed and said, "Oh, there were so many girls after them". When asked about her garage apartment in College Park she replied that she had never seen any reason to move.

The small crop-dusting operation that was formed to eradicate the boll weevil infestation in southern cotton fields grew to become one of the world's largest airlines.

Miss FitzGerald was buried in the St. Mary Catholic Church Cemetery, Ogdensburg, New York.

The Expansion Continues

David C Garrett Jr. joined Delta in 1946 as a reservation agent. He became president in 1971 and was Delta's CEO from 1978 until his retirement in 1987. He remained on the board until 1994. He was the very embodiment of Delta - a keeper of its invaluable traditions, but also a leader who led the expansion into the Western U.S., elevating the airline into a powerful national carrier. It was during Dave's tenure that the people of Delta gave a B-767 named, "The Spirit of Delta", to the company, a perfect symbol of what make's Delta unique. That gift also represents the continuing trust and respect at every level of the company that is Dave's special legacy. What a gentleman!

Delta purchased Chicago and Southern Air Lines in 1953 and flew under the name Delta-C&S for the next two years. This added a north-south network from Chicago and Detroit to Houston and New Orleans – and Delta's first international route, New Orleans to Caracas via Havana. The network expanded to Washington, DC, and New York in 1956. Delta initially flew only to

Newark, but between 1957 and 1958 the airline added flights to Idlewild, which was later renamed to John F. Kennedy International (JFK). Delta had no direct flights between the Northeast and Florida until it merged with Northeast Airlines in 1972. Trans-Atlantic service began in 1978 with the first nonstop service from Atlanta to London.

With the arrival of the jet age in 1960, the hangers were no longer useful, so Delta built an immense Jet Base (located at today's Technical Operations Center). Hangars 1 and 2 were used as a secondary maintenance location for Delta jets until the mid-1980s, then the old hangars were used only for storage by the surrounding offices. In 1995, the non-profit Delta Air Transport Heritage Museum was founded and moved into the historic hangars. The B-767 named "The Spirit of Delta", which was purchased by Delta employees for the company, sits proudly in one of the old hangers. Ship 41, a restored DC-3 sits in the other hanger along with a Travel Air and a replica of the "Puffer"

Delta's domestic operation continued to expand as it merged with Western Airlines in 1987. In the 1990s, Delta purchased the European assets of defunct Pan American World Airways, which greatly enlarged its international operation. On April 14, 2008, both Delta and Northwest Airlines announced that they would merge under the Delta name. The merger gave Delta a strong Asia Pacific presence.

C.E. Woolman, the founder of Delta, once said, "No one person is an airline. An airline is a team". His philosophy has remained the cornerstone of Delta's success. Every employee is made to feel they are an important part of the team.

Some of the information about the early days of Delta was obtained from the book "Delta The History of an Airline" by W. David Lewis and Wesley Phillips Newton that was published in 1979 by the University of Georgia Press in Athens, Georgia. Other information was gathered from newspaper articles published in the Atlanta Constitution newspaper. The newspaper information was gathered from the Newspaper.com website.

Chapter 2
Dr. Janus' Rocking Chair

In February of 1966, my wife Carol was working at the Delta Air Lines General Office in the Revenue Accounting department. She was a stewardess for Eastern Airlines when we first met in 1962, but "stews" could not be married at the time, so she had to quit. In those days, all stewardesses were young, unmarried, and slim. They were required to keep their weight within prescribed limits, and they were weighed in before each flight. Typical employment ads for stewardesses stated that they should be thin and petite, weighing between 100 and 128 pounds and standing between 5'2" and 5'6".

The military style stewardess uniform consisted of a skirt, blouse, jacket with brass button, high-heel shoes, leather pocketbooks, and a pill-box hat. Some airlines required stewardesses to wear a girdle as part of their uniform. The uniforms typically cost employees over $100, which was a considerable amount of money at the time. They could have the money deducted from their paychecks each month.

After graduating from high school, my first job was with Eastern Airlines as a Ticket Agent. I had never flown in an airplane before, but I was hooked after my first ride in a DC-7 from Atlanta to Miami. This began a lifelong love of aviation. I enrolled in flight school at the Fulton County Airport in Atlanta and begin to devote my time and money toward the dream of becoming a pilot. Then

I met Carol. We got married and had a child. My dream was put on hold.

In the early sixties, the airlines were rapidly expanding and there was a shortage of pilots. Carol and I decided that I should go back to flying and pursue my dream. She went to work for Delta Air Lines, and I went back to flight school. Four years later, I was working the midnight shift in the Ramp Tower for Eastern Airlines and was a part-time Flight Instructor at the Fulton County Airport during the day. Somehow, I managed a few hours' sleep in between jobs.

One morning the telephone woke me from a deep sleep. It was Carol, talking a mile-a-minute. I said, "Slow down, I can't understand a word you're saying". She took a deep breath, "You've been hired by Delta as a pilot and your training class starts next month". In disbelief, I asked, "How do you know"? She said that her supervisor had told her. He asked if she would like to call me with the news and offered to let her continue working while I attended the 3-month initial training class. She would have to keep the information secret. At the time, Delta had a strict anti-nepotism policy. We both knew that it would be impossible for us to keep the information secret. She gave her two-weeks' notice.

The next month, I walked into the classroom on Virginia Avenue in Hapeville, Georgia, to begin initial training as a pilot for Delta. In our class of thirty pilots I was one of the youngest, at age 23. Our instructor, Frost Ward, gave us a hearty welcome, "Gentlemen, you are starting a career that will one day earn you as much as twenty-five thousand dollars per year, as a Delta captain, if you can make it through the next three months." Wow, $25,000 a year! Our starting salary at the time was $475 per month.

For the next three months, we ate, slept, and breathed the Douglas Aircraft Company's DC-6 and DC-7. The ground school instructors, who were former Delta mechanics, knew the airplanes inside and out. They taught us everything we needed to know to become Certified Flight Engineers.

Dr. Janus

Part of the hiring process for Delta pilots involved a psychiatric interview with Dr. Janus. Delta relied heavily on his recommendation. When entering Dr. Janus' office, pilots were offered a seat in a rocking chair. Prospective pilots were obsessed about the rocking chair. It was universally assumed that the rocking chair was a test. Did you rock continuously, which might indicate anxiety? Did you rock intermittently, perhaps indicating flexibility? If you rocked in response to a question, did that mean the question hit a nerve?

Finally, after many years, someone found the courage to ask, "What's the deal with this rocking chair?" Dr. Janus is said to have told him the rocking chair was there because his wife disliked it and didn't want it in the house, but she thought it would look nice in his office. Thousands of pilots were terrified by the interview with Dr. Janus. To this day, many pilots still question the significance of the rocking chair in his office.

After graduation, we got our uniforms and our names were placed on the pilot seniority list. I think Delta had around 750 pilots at the time. Compare that to the over 15,000 pilots today!

Atlanta was home base for my entire career with Delta, but I was assigned TDY (temporary duty) in Chicago for a month after finishing initial training. Chicago had a crew base, but they needed additional flight engineers until the next class graduated. I was given a schedule flying to St. Louis and back 4 days per week. We stayed at a motel near the airport in Des Plains that mostly catered to airline crews. I spent the entire month lying around a large swimming pool and playing beach volleyball on a sandy area next to the pool. Could this be real? At end of the month, I returned home to Atlanta.

Sin City

The Atlanta based employees were a close-knit group. We quickly made lots of new friends. Many of the single employees lived in apartments located near the airport in an area that was affectionately known as "Sin City". Most of the married employees lived in subdivisions around the airport. We worked together, went to church together, bowled together, partied together, and our children all played little league sports together. It really was a family!

On any given afternoon, if you went into John Henry's barber shop in College Park you might just find yourself sitting in the chair next to Mr. Dave Garrett, President of Delta. Everyone got a haircut at John Henry's. Any establishment in southwest Atlanta would gladly take a check written on the Delta Credit Union. Merchants knew that Delta Air Lines did not tolerate employees bouncing checks. This was a strict no-no!

Sin City was located just west of the Atlanta Airport, within the city limits of College Park. The apartment buildings in the 40-block area housed many single airline employees in the 1960s and 1970s. The area, bounded by Virginia Avenue to the north, East Main Street to the west, Columbia Avenue to the south, and I-85 on the east, was convenient to the airport, so many of the new hire flight attendants didn't own a car. The Hanger Cab Company provided an inexpensive alternative.

Two Delta captains, Dana Jones and Jim Carlton, owned apartment complexes in the area. Captain Jones would attend new-hire classes and pitch his apartments located at the corner of Virginia Avenue and East Main Street. This complex, known as Airlane, is now called Virginia Street Manor and still stands on the corner.

In 1966, the salary for new-hire pilots was $475 per month during their probation period. Agents, mechanics, flight attendants and other airline employees made a similar amount, so most of the single employees had at least one roommate to make ends meet.

Harvard House, at the corner of Harvard Ave and Adams Street, was one of the most infamous of the "airline apartments". There was always a party going on at the Harvard House. These apartments are still standing today. Columbia Apartments at the corner of Myrtle Street and Columbia Avenue was also a swinging place. On several weekends during the summer, the manager would host a beach party.

The apartment complex was at the end of Columbia Avenue, so the area was blocked off by the police and sand was spread on the street. The Carling Brewing Company was located on the south expressway just north of the airport. They would bring a refrigerated truck with "beer taps" on the side to provide refreshments for the party. And a band or two would perform until the wee hours of the morning. The Columbia apartments were torn down when I-85 was relocated to make room for a new east-west runway on the north side of the airport.

Carol lived at these apartments, with two other roommates, when she first came to Atlanta as a stewardess for Eastern Airlines in 1961. She and her roommates had barely unpacked their bags at the Columbia Apartments before a salesman showed up at their door wanting to sell them a set of waterless cookware. They told him they did not have the money and were not interested, but he offered to demonstrate the cookware by preparing dinner for them. You guessed it, before the night was over, they had signed a contract to purchase a set of cookware on monthly installments.

As I remember, the total cost of the cookware was more than their monthly salary. He prayed on all the new-hire flight attendants moving into the apartments in Sin City. I am quite sure the managers of the apartments must have gotten a cut for tipping him off whenever a new customer moved into one of the apartments.

Like most stewardesses at the time, Carol had a closet with shoe boxes filled with the little miniature whiskey bottles from the airplane liquor kits. More shoe boxes were filled with the Winston three-cigarette packs that were provided on the airplane meal trays.

What a fabulous time to be single and employed by one of the airlines in Atlanta.

Air Host Inn

The iconic motel on Virginia Avenue was the center of airline social activity in Sin City. It sat at the entrance to the new Atlanta Jet Age terminal that opened on May 3, 1961. For many years, it was home to new-hire Delta "stewardesses" during their initial training. The motel featured 150 luxury rooms, swimming pool, patio, Three Hearths Restaurant, and the Cloud 9 Lounge. The numerous meeting rooms and banquet facilities were frequently used by Delta Air Lines. The Airline Pilots Association held their monthly meetings at the motel. The biggest event ever held at the Air Host Inn was the retirement party for Captain Thomas Prioleau "Pre" Ball, Vice President of Flight Operations. It was hosted by the Airline Pilots Association in 1971. Captain Pre Ball was loved and respected by the pilot group that a presented him with a new BMW sports car, purchased with contributions from individual pilots. "Pre" was inducted into the Georgia Aviation Hall of Fame in 2005 and died in 2006 at age 99.

Chapter 3
The Second Officer

All newly hired pilots with Delta started out as flight engineers. Delta preferred the term Second Officer since we were hired to be pilots. The flight engineer's seat was merely a starting position. Some airlines used professional flight engineers, who were former mechanics and did not have a pilot's license. They remained flight engineers for their entire career.

As airliners developed into larger, multi-engine aircraft, it became necessary to add a cockpit crew member to manage the complex systems in use. This was especially true with early piston and jet engines, as they required much more input and monitoring.

With advances in modern technology, the need for a flight engineer has been all but eliminated in the modern-day airliner design.

Flight engineers were responsible for operating and monitoring the hydraulic, pressurization, fuel, electrical and air conditioning systems. On the DC-6 and DC-7 they accomplished this from a seat in the cockpit, which was a fold-down jump seat between the pilots. In later years, the flight engineers' position was behind the pilots, in a seat situated in front of a panel with the controls and gauges for the systems they monitored.

The Douglas DC-6 was a piston-powered airliner built from 1946 to 1958. Originally built as a military transport, it was reworked after the war to compete with the Lockheed Constellation in the long-range commercial transport market. Fast and pressurized, it could compete with Eastern Airlines' Lockheed Constellations between Chicago and Miami. The DC-6 carried 50 passengers plus it had a Sky Lounge in the back of the plane that would accommodate six people in comfort. Delta invited customers to "join your friends for quiet conversation, cards or coffee, in the luxurious atmosphere of an exclusive club." It was the first Douglas aircraft to exceed a 300 miles-per-hour cruise speed.

Delta promoted its DC-6 fleet as "None Faster - None Finer to and Through the South." It was Delta's first pressurized and air-conditioned aircraft. A thermal or "heated wing" deicing system allowed for greater all-weather dependability. The DC-6 was the first Delta aircraft with reverse propellers. When landing with reverse propellers, the pitch of the propellers reversed, so that they pushed air forward instead of backwards, allowing safer and shorter landings on wet and dry runways and reduced taxi time. It was Delta's first aircraft with seat tray tables. On earlier planes, passengers balanced meal trays on pillows held on their laps. Delta briefly flew the DC-6 with two pilots, but federal regulations changed soon after Delta launched service to require a third pilot in the cockpit—a flight engineer.

The Douglas DC-7, which came later, was faster, had a longer range, and could cruise above the weather at 25,000 feet. It was the first commercial aircraft able to fly non-stop westbound across the United States against the jet stream. With a top speed of 410 miles per hour, it was the fastest piston-powered commercial airplane in 1954. The DC-7 cruise speed was 25 to 30 mph faster than the Douglas DC-6 and Lockheed Constellation. The longer length of the DC-7 fuselage (over eight feet more than the DC-6), allowed room for an eight-passenger Sky Room, with facing seats, and a five-seat Sky Lounge, in addition to two main cabins. Delta launched industry-leading, luxury Royal Crown Service with the DC-7 in 1958. Royal Service flights featured: Three flight attendants (instead of the usual two) for the finest and the swiftest service available; Complimentary champagne; A choice of entrées at mealtime, and canapés and cocktails in the afternoon; Muzak tape recordings played during boarding; Children received Delta's first "kiddie wings" souvenir pins (Junior Pilot pins for boys and Junior Stewardess pins for girls); and, at the airport, Royal Service customers had a special check-in desk.

The Second Officer (flight engineer) on the DC-6 and DC-7 was responsible for starting the large piston engines. The engine start control switches were on an overhead panel, so this required the S/O to stand up and lean forward to reach the switches. Operating the switches required the use of three fingers on one hand, while the other hand was used to engage the fuel lever at just the right moment. If the switches and levers were not moved in concert, the engine would backfire, sending out plumes of black smoke and a ball of fire.

I remember a "senior stewardess" on my first or second flight (she was probably in her late twenties), who delighted in breaking in a new S/O fresh out of school. Betty Warren would stand behind him, as he started the engines. Just at the right time, she would "goose" the S/O, which usually caused just enough of a distraction that the switches and the fuel control levers were not engaged properly. You guessed it! Betty would grin from ear to ear as the engine coughed loudly and sent black smoke and fire out the tailpipes. Passengers in window seats would gasp at the sight. Then she would get on the PA, in her British accent, and assure everyone, "Everything is okay, we have a new S/O on-board today and he will soon get the hang of starting the engines"! She taught me to always watch my six (guard your rear)! We remain good friends even today!

In the summer of 1966, Northwest Airlines found fatigue cracks in the fuselage of the DC-6, so the FAA ordered that all the aircraft had to be flown unpressurized until they were inspected for cracks. This meant that we had to fly below 10,000 feet. In the summertime, flying through the cumulus clouds that were found at the lower cruising altitudes made for a bumpy ride. In addition, the air conditioning system on the DC-6 could not sufficiently cool the cabin in the summertime. During a long taxi for takeoff it was not unusual for the temperature in the cabin to approach 100 degrees. The passengers, who boarded in coats and ties, were quickly getting rid of this attire. After becoming airborne, the hot temperatures and bumpy ride meant that the burp bags in the seatback pockets would soon be put to good use.

Chapter 4

Ohio and Mississippi Valleys

Many of the cities served by the DC-6, DC-7 and CV-440 were in the Ohio and Mississippi River valleys or the southeastern part of the United States. If the weather was good, flying between some of these cities was often conducted under VFR conditions (visual flight rules). Navigation was done by flying over recognizable landmarks on the ground instead of following prescribed routes using on-board radio equipment. Captains had to be airport qualified into each of the airports that was served by the type of airplane he flew. He was required to ride the jump-seat into each of these airports as part of his initial checkout as Captain. This would be completely impossible today considering Delta's expansive route system that serves 300 destinations, in 60 countries, across all six inhabited continents.

Most of the captains were former WWII pilots, with lots of experience under their belt. Flight operations were not nearly as standardized in those days. Newly hired pilots kept a log of how each captain "ran his cockpit" and shared the information with other new hires. I learned a wealth of information from those "old WWII guys". Most of them were likely in their forties or fifties since the mandatory retirement age was 60.

My first copilot position, or First Officer as Delta preferred, was on the CV-440 – a twin-engine aircraft that carried 44 passengers and one stewardess.

Passengers sometimes refer to the copilot as a co-captain, but there is only one Captain of the aircraft. The airplane did not have an autopilot, so one pilot flew while the other handled the radio communications. Mechanical and weather delays were quite commonplace in those days. The piston engines were not nearly as reliable as the jet engines and the landing minimums were much higher at many of the smaller airports that lacked sophisticated equipment. In the wintertime, a snowstorm moving across the Midwest would cause havoc with Delta's schedule for days. Many times, I arrived home a couple of days later than scheduled. The passengers, dressed in suits and ties, seemed to understand, and took things in stride. Flying was still something unique. Many of our passenger were the rich and famous.

Snowy Day in Fort Wayne

One winter day, we landed in Fort Wayne, Indiana with a light snow falling. We taxied up to the parking spot, where passengers were lined up behind a fence waiting to board. There were no jetways at the time. Passengers had to walk across the ramp and climb stairs to board the plane. I notice a well-dressed couple saying their goodbyes. A few minutes later, the passengers were all on board and we taxied toward the runway for takeoff. The stewardess came to the cockpit and told us that one of the passengers was terrified of flying and wanted off the airplane. I went back to reassure him that everything was okay. He was an attorney and had an important business meeting in Detroit. He told me his wife was concerned about him driving to Detroit and insisted that he fly. However, he could not overcome his fear of flying and needed to deplane. We taxied back to the gate and the man in the dark gray suit walked down the steps with tears in his eyes. His wife was still waiting behind the fence. She must have known that her husband wouldn't be able to overcome his fear of flying. I felt so sorry for this man!

Lindale AC

Crews flying into Detroit stayed downtown at the Cadillac Hotel. Located in an alley near the hotel, Lindale AC was a favorite among airline crews. For half a century, the legendary Lindell AC bar was a mecca for visiting athletes, sports fans, hometown heroes, and media personalities who would feast on burgers, fries, onion rings, stories and a "favorite drink", while surrounded by wall to wall photographs and museum quality sports memorabilia. The USA Today once crowned it the "number one sports bar in America." Carl's Chop House was a favorite for fine dining, but most crew members didn't eat there very often. Lindell AC was more our style! Sometime later, the flight crews begin laying over in Ann Arbor. I think the move occurred in the early seventies. Everyone enjoyed staying in the little artsy-fartsy town.

Rawhide

The Executive Inn was the layover hotel in Evansville, Indiana. Originally a Ramada Inn, the motel was purchased in 1967 by Robert Green and his wife Mary

Agnes, who managed the day to day operations. They enlarged it to include a 10-story wing in 1972. Some of the best-known rock and roll performers of the day appeared in the riverfront hotel Showroom Lounge. These included: Little Richard, Jerry Lee Lewis, Fats Domino and many more. For each show, Mary Agnes reserved a table right in front of the stage for the Delta crew – all free! On one layover, I saw Frankie Lane sing Rawhide – the theme song for the tv series of the same name.

The Miracle Mile

The layover hotels in Chicago changed many times over the years, but the longer layovers were usually in hotels around Rush Street, near the lakefront. In the 1960s, Rush Street was the center of the Chicago nightlife as home to many great cabarets, bars, clubs, and restaurants. The Chicago Sun-Times described it as the "hippest strip" in Chicago. What a great place to layover! I loved the Chicago-style deep-dish pizza.

Hammerin' Hank

Early Cincinnati layovers were at a hotel located on the west side of Walnut Street between 4th and 5th Street. The Gibson Hotel was first built in 1849. Several buildings were destroyed by fire and torn down. The third building of 12 stories was enlarged in 1922 to become one of the largest hotels in the Midwest, with 1000 rooms. It became the Sheraton Gibson in 1950, when the Sheraton Corporation bought the building. It was finally closed in 1974 and was razed in 1977.

The Braves baseball team moved to Atlanta in 1966, the year I started flying for Delta. One of my first trips was a baseball charter to Cincinnati for the Braves organization. We stayed at the Gibson Hotel, along with the team and two of their sluggers: Eddie Mathews and Hank Aaron. Who knew that "Hammerin' Hank" would go on to break the lifetime home run record of Babe Ruth in 1974?

The Peabody Ducks

The layover hotel in Memphis was the Peabody. Yes, the one with the ducks in the lobby fountain. The Rendezvous was the favorite crew restaurant. It is still going strong today. Their website tells the story: "For over 70 years, the Vergos family has been serving their signature dry rub ribs in a basement through a downtown alley across from the Peabody Hotel. And while the world outside has changed considerably, little has changed in that alley basement." Best ribs I've ever had! That was the only place I ever ate in Memphis!

Savannah Airport Graves

One of the small airports on Delta's route system was unique. Few of the passengers who fly in and out of the Savannah, Georgia Airport (SAV) notice two peculiar rectangles lying in the middle of the runway. What appears at first glance to be patches from repair work in the runway are the headstones of Richard and Catherine Dotson - the only known graves to be embedded in an airport runway in the world.

The story behind how the husband and wife came to rest in the middle of the bustling runway begins in 1877, long before Wilbur and Orville Wright first took flight in 1903. That's the year Catherine died, after a lifetime spent farming her family's land on the outskirts of Savannah, back when it was called Cherokee Hills. Richard, her husband of 50 years, died seven years later, and the couple was buried side-by-side in a family cemetery that had about 100 graves, including those of slaves.

They rested peacefully until the Savannah Airport began work on an extension to Runway 10 during WWII. The new runway would extend straight through the Dotsons' plot. The descendants allowed officials to relocate most of the graves, but they insisted that the patriarch and matriarch should not be disturbed, claiming that they would have wanted to stay on the land they worked so hard to cultivate and purchase. Two more graves, of their relatives Daniel Hueston and John Dotson, can be found nearby in the brush.

Since it's illegal to transfer remains without consent from next of kin, the airport simply paved over them. Although they didn't have to, the airport chose to honor the Dotson Family by placing two headstones over their graves that lay flat with the 9,350-foot runway. Family members are still escorted to safely visit them, but they cannot leave flowers.

It is said that if you are landing in SAV just after sundown, two figures will appear just along the north side of the runway. I never saw any figures beside the runway, but I landed on the headstones of Catherine and Richard many times. During taxi for takeoff, I would sometimes make a PA and tell passengers about the uniqueness of this runway.

Chapter 5
Gone With The Wind

On December 13, 1940, Captain Charles Dolson, First Officer Raymond Nelson, and Stewardess Bertie Perkins left Nashville, Tennessee at 7:30 pm on a chartered flight for Atlanta. Bertie was a small-town girl from Vernon, Alabama, and the first stewardess hired by Delta. The flight departed 14 hours later than scheduled. It was bringing "Scarlett", Vivien Leigh to Atlanta for the anniversary premiere of Gone With The Wind. It was the final leg of the transcontinental flight that had started in Los Angeles on American Airways. Weather delays in El Paso and Dallas, Texas had increased the 16-hour trip to 28 hours. Also, along on the flight was Alfred Hitchcock, famed English director; Laurence Olivier; and Miss Hazel Rogers, hairdresser, and cosmetician.

During this time, aviation was a patchwork of regional airlines serving different sections of the country. Routes were controlled by the government. A cross country flight would require connecting flights on several different airlines. The group flew American Airways from LA to Nashville, where they connected to the Delta charter flight to Atlanta, to attend the anniversary celebration scheduled for the next day. A reporter on the flight wrote a detailed account of the events.

Numb with fatigue after 30 hours of battling weather to reach the Atlanta premiere party on time, they were finally overhead the Atlanta Municipal Airport at about 9:00 pm. The weather had deteriorated and the ceiling in Atlanta had dropped to 300 feet. Captain Dolson made a couple of instrument approaches in a failed attempt to land, before informing the movie stars that they were proceeding to their alternate airport in Augusta, Georgia. Miss Leigh suggested that they go back to Nashville, where they could make connections to Los Angeles, and asked "Could we radio a message to the Atlanta branch of the British War Relief Society and tell them how disappointed they were in not being able to make the appearance". Birdie Perkins called the cockpit and was informed that the weather conditions had worsened in Nashville, and their only option was to proceed to Augusta.

The flight departed Augusta at 10:30 the next morning and started fighting the weather all over again as the plane encountered turbulence on the way to Atlanta. Alfred Hitchcock had the hopeless feeling that the flight would be unable to land again and that thought crept through the plane. Laurence Olivier asked Captain Dolson to leave the cockpit door open, "so he could see what they were doing". First Officer Nelson and Stewardess Perkins assured everyone they would be able to land in Atlanta, but Miss Leigh was skeptical. A picture in the Atlanta newspaper showed Birdie trying to protect her famous passenger from the drizzling rain, which greeted them at the municipal airport, along with a small crowd of stout-hearted fans.

Cockpit to Chairman

It was the 1st anniversary of the premiere of the film and the star was returning to Atlanta for the anniversary celebration. On Friday, December 15, 1939, the city was abuzz with excitement. Spotlights swept the sky with huge beacons of light. Peachtree at Pryor Street was closed to traffic. An enormous crowd, numbering 300,000 people according to the Atlanta Constitution, lined the streets on this ice-cold night in Atlanta. Car after car paused at Lowe's Grand Theater as the stars came out. Wild cheers greeted each celebrity as they braved the cold to participate in a brief radio interview. Noticeably absent were Hattie McDaniel (Mammy) and Butterfly McQueen (Prissy), black actresses with major roles who were not welcome in the white side of the segregated Atlanta society. Noticeably present was a young Martin Luther King, Jr., who sang in a "negro boys' choir" from his father's church, Ebenezer Baptist. In 1978, the Loew's Grand was gutted by fire. In 1982 Georgia-Pacific built its headquarters on the site.

Captain Dolson, was hired by Delta in 1935 and was promoted to Chief Pilot about one year after this flight. He had a long and distinguished career with Delta Air Lines, before retiring as the Chairman of the Board, and Chief Executive Office of the airline in 1971, as the only pilot in the company history to go from the cockpit to the highest executive position with the company.

Information about the Gone With The Wind flight was obtained from newspaper articles published in the Atlanta Constitution newspaper. The newspaper information was gathered from the Newspaper.com website.

Chapter 6
Gone But Not Forgotten

No profession has as much "skin in the game," as do pilots. If a doctor makes a serious mistake, a patient may unnecessarily die. If a lawyer makes a serious mistake, an innocent client may go to jail. Professionals are subject to review boards, but they rarely lift a professional's license. Pilots, though, are subject to the constant review of the uncompromising authority of gravity. If a pilot makes a serious mistake, gravity ends - not only the pilot's career - but his or her life.

Before Flight Simulators

In 1967, the Hilton Inn, across the street from the New Orleans Moisant Airport, was used for short layovers by Delta. Just after midnight, Delta Flight 9877 took off on a training flight with a captain and several flight engineer trainees. They were attempting to execute a simulated two-engine out approach when the aircraft hit power lines approximately 2,300 feet short of the runway threshold. It cut a swath of destruction through a residential area near the airport and crashed into the rear of the Hilton Inn. On board the jet was five pilots and an inspector for the Federal Aviation Agency. All died in the crash. The pilots included New Orleans Chief Pilot, Captain Maurice Watson, 45; Captain James Morton, 47; and Flight Engineers George Piazza II, 36; William Jeter Jr, 33; and Davey Posey, 25. The FAA Inspector from Houston was William Snow. Nine teenage girls on a high-school senior trip with 23 of their friends were killed in the hotel. An employee of the hotel died in the boiler room and two other people died when the plane sliced through their home.

The NTSB determined the probable cause of this accident was the improper supervision by the instructor, and the improper use of flight and power controls by both the instructor and the captain-trainee during a simulated two-engine out landing approach, which resulted in a loss of control.

Delta lost two other aircraft during training accidents. A brand-new, four million dollar, Convair 880 stalled and crashed during takeoff in Atlanta in May of 1960. Delta identified the victims as Captain James Longino, 41, College Park, Ga; Captain H.L. Lube, 45, College Park; First Officer Bryan Bolt of Atlanta; and Captain W. F. Williams, 50, from Miami.

A DC-9 crashed during a training flight at the Greater Southwest International Airport, in Ft. Worth, in May of 1972. Delta flight 9570 began to oscillate about the roll axis after crossing the runway threshold during a landing approach, then rolled rapidly to the right and struck the runway with the right wing low. This crash was attributed to Wake Turbulence behind a McDonnell Douglas DC-10 that made a touch-and-go landing ahead of it.

The plane's occupants consisted of three pilots and an FAA inspector, all of whom were killed in the crash and subsequent fire. The victims were Captain George Gray, 35, an instructor pilot based in Atlanta; Captain Franklin Cook, 32, who was transferring from Dallas to

Atlanta; Captain Johnny Martin, 35, of Dallas, and FAA examiner Leon Hull, 38, of Fort Worth.

The resulting investigation prompted changes to the minimum distance that aircraft must keep when following "heavy" aircraft to avoid Wake Turbulence.

In the early days of flight, this disturbance of air was called "prop wash" – wind created by the spinning propellers. Although the vortices off the wingtips were recognized as turbulence, they were not completely understood by most people in the aviation community. It was the introduction in 1970 of the larger wide-bodied "jumbo" jets with much stronger vortices that led to an effort by the FAA, NASA, the Air Force, and the commercial aviation community to study the growing wake vortex phenomena and establish safe operational distances between similar and dissimilar size aircraft.

Data accumulated by the vortex studies contributed to a broader understanding of these dangerous wakes of turbulent air that trail behind every aircraft, and helped the Federal Aviation Administration (FAA) establish safe separation distances between various sizes of aircraft during takeoff and landing operations, and also during cruise flight.

In the seventies, the airlines turned to newly designed aircraft simulators to conduct initial training of its pilots. A flight simulator is a device used for flight training that artificially re-creates aircraft flight and the environment in which it flies. It can safely be used to train pilots for any emergency that is likely to happen.

Today, the Delta Aircrew Training Center in Atlanta operates a fleet of 37 Full Flight Simulators in 9 different categories of aircraft. After training on a new aircraft, the pilots' first landing in the actual airplane will be on their first scheduled passenger flight.

Wind-shear and Microburst

One of the most tragic accidents in Delta's history occurred in August of 1985. An L-1011, operating as Delta flight 191, crashed and killed 137 people and injured 28 others, while landing at the Dallas-Fort Worth airport. Flight 191 departed Fort Lauderdale in the mid-afternoon. In the cockpit were Captain Edward Connors, First Officer Rudolph Price and Second Officer Nick Nassick.

A weak frontal system across Texas began to provide the needed trigger for thunderstorm development. Just before 6 p.m., a shower developed near the airport, but it was not a cause for concern. As the L-1011 neared the airport, the previously innocuous shower began to intensify. Just 1,500 feet above the ground, on final approach and just 1 minute from landing, Captain Connors noted lightning in the cloud ahead of them. Despite the impending storm, the weather report from the airport was not ominous and was well within the restrictions for landing.

Just seconds later, at 800 feet above the ground as the plane entered the thunderstorm, a series of rapid events conspired to doom the jet. First the plane accelerated, hit from behind by strong winds. Then, just as suddenly, the plane rapidly lost speed and altitude. The pilots responded by pushing the throttles to a maximum power setting, but it was too late. Without any altitude left, the plane smacked into the ground and ran across a highway, killing a motorist. It plowed into two water towers and burst into flames, just thousands of feet from the runway. All three of the cockpit crew members died in the crash. Miraculously, three of the eight flight attendants and 29 passengers survived.

How could an aircraft only 800 feet from the ground and seconds from landing crash so violently with no warning? After a lengthy investigation, the NTSB concluded that wind-shear and a microburst encountered in the thunderstorm caused the pilots to lose control of their plane. Although the effects of wind shear were known by pilots, microbursts had been studied less and pilots had only limited training. In addition, real-time wind shear information was not readily available to pilots.

As thunderstorms gather strength, they produce turbulent winds. These violent gusts are unpredictable and can bring down an airplane in the right circumstances. In the case of Delta 191, the pilots were not aware of the severity of the wind-shear and potential downburst that was directly in their flight path. In the aftermath of this tragedy, NASA developed sophisticated airborne wind-shear detection systems that pilots could use while in-flight.

This was an exciting period of growth for Delta Air Lines, as jets replaced the old piston airplanes, but it was somewhat tragic at times.

The National Transportation Safety Board (NTSB) is an independent Federal agency charged by Congress with investigating every civil aviation accident in the United States. The NTSB makes public its actions and decisions through accident reports that provide details about the accident, analysis of the factual data, conclusions and the probable cause of the accident, and the related safety recommendations. Information about these accidents was obtained from their website.

Chapter 7

Remembering Captain Cushing

A Delta DC-3, NC-49657, flown by 48-year-old Captain George Cushing, departed Macon, Georgia at 10:04 am. All the passengers were Delta officials, who were making a survey of airport facilities for a new alternate route between Atlanta and Savanna. Most of the officials were under forty years of age. The DC-3 was scheduled for a stop in Columbus, Georgia before flying back to Atlanta. The aircraft reported over Columbus at 10:34 am and was observed circling the Muscogee County Airport in preparation for landing.

At 10:30 am, J.C. Fussell, a private pilot, departed from the Columbus Municipal Airport in his BT-13 (modified Army trainer). He arrived in the vicinity of the Muscogee County Airport at the same time as the Delta aircraft entered the traffic pattern for landing. The BT-13 approached from the southeast and made a long shallow turn to the right onto final approach for landing on Runway 5.

After entering the traffic pattern, the DC-3 made a one and one-half circles to the left around the airport; and then, turned left onto final approach for a landing on Runway 5. Upon completion of the turn, the BT-13 was above and slightly to the right of the Delta plane. It would have been extremely difficult for Captain Cushing to have seen the BT-13 and to determine the intentions of the pilot. The absence of a control tower made it important that all traffic conform to the established pattern, but four witnesses testified that the BT-13 was flying contrary to the direction of traffic.

The Delta flight was approximately 10 feet above the ground when the BT-13 descended onto the empennage of the DC-3, just ahead of the rudder and vertical fin. An immediate application of power was made by Captain Cushing, as the tail of the aircraft was forced down from the collision. The BT-13 remained lodged on the tail surfaces of the DC-3 as it climbed to approximately 150 feet above the runway. Both aircraft then crashed to the ground and burned. It took over an hour to extinguish the flames since no mobile fire or crash equipment was located at the Muscogee County Airport. The flames made it impossible to rescue any of the victims.

This was the first airplane crash in Delta's history. The weather during the entire morning of the accident was good. At the time of the crash, there were high, thin, scattered clouds and the visibility was 9 miles. The safety board determined that the probable cause of this accident was the failure of the pilot in the BT-13 to fly a standard left-hand pattern in his approach to the airport and to keep a diligent lookout for other traffic.

Delta Family Days

Delta experienced tremendous growth between 1949 and 1952. Net earnings soared from record-setting profits of $639,444 in 1949 to an unheard-of amount of $1,650,450 in 1952. During this period, the number of employees increased from 2,093 to 2,722. "The family seems to get larger all the time, and it isn't as easy as it once was to know everybody," the company magazine noted as employees celebrated Delta Family Day. They had just experienced the most successful winter season in the company's history.

Pat Godfrey, a Delta Air Lines aircraft inspector, was inspired by a newspaper article he read about an Atlanta industrial firm's recreational site on Georgia's Allatoona Lake. He called upon C. E. Woolman, the founder and then president of Delta Air Lines who enthusiastically endorsed a similar project as a weekend escape for employees. The desire to foster a sense of togetherness, amid the rapid expansion, set in motion a "grass-roots" effort to acquire a track of land at nearby Allatoona Lake to be used by Delta employees for boating, fishing, picnicking, and other recreational activities.

Cushing Park

A 35-acre recreation area, located on the shores of Lake Allatoona, was purchased and named in honor of George R. Cushing, the former Vice President of Operations for Delta Air Lines, who lost his life in the midair collision with a small aircraft at Columbus, Georgia. Developed by Delta Air Lines employees, and incorporated in 1952, the park is located 1 hour north of the Atlanta Airport, off I-575 between Canton and Woodstock, Georgia. The park played an important role in the social lives of the Delta family for many years.

During the late sixties and early seventies, I took my family to Cushing Park many times. The cinder-block cabins could be rented for a very reasonable fee. The park also leased parking pads, where several employees used mobile homes as a weekend retreat. The company really felt like an extended family and going to Cushing Park on weekends was just like attending a family reunion. Because of the size the Delta organization had attained by 1977, some long- cherished customs were reluctantly discontinued. Cushing Memorial Park was no longer large enough to accommodate the Delta Day outing, which was once held every summer for employees and their families. A yearly "Delta Night at the Braves", at which personnel from all over the system could come to Atlanta to watch their National League baseball team was instituted as a partial substitute. More important, a series of annual award observances for employees and who had reached significant milestones in their service would be invited to the Atlanta's World Congress Center, where the employee and their spouse would be entertained at Delta's expense, concluding with a banquet. As Delta continued to grow, these traditions would soon disappear as well.

The recreational area was originally built by employees of Delta Air Lines along the lines of a private club and membership was limited to employees and retirees of Delta. The facility was spun off some years ago, but the name Cushing Memorial Park remains.

Information about the crash of NC-49657 was obtained from the official Civil Aeronautics Board report that was released on August 1, 1947. Information about Cushing Park was gathered from articles published in the Atlanta Constitution newspaper. The newspaper information was gathered from the Newspaper.com website.

Chapter 8
The Times They Were A'Changin'

Delta was named as one of the Best Workplaces for Diversity in 2019, an honor the airline had earned for four years running. Delta Air Lines started in the twenties as a small regional carrier mainly serving the southeastern part of the United States. After WWII, the airline started expanding north, south, and in 1961 was awarded a couple of routes to the west coast from Atlanta. During this period, many other changes were occurring in America.

Marlon Green, a U.S. Air Force pilot, applied for a job with Continental Airlines in 1957, only to be denied employment after the airline discovered he was black. Green's subsequent lawsuit led to a 1963 U.S. Supreme Court decision that found he was the victim of discrimination. The landmark ruling broke the color barrier for commercial pilots, and the following year, American Airlines became the first commercial airline to hire a black pilot.

The Civil Rights Act of 1964 outlawed segregation and discrimination in public accommodations and forbid employers to discriminate against minorities. Delta hired Pat Murphy, its first African American flight attendant, two years later, in 1966. This was such a news-worthy event that Delta's Vice President of Flight Operations, Captain "Snake" Smith asked to address the monthly meeting of the Air Line Pilots Association (ALPA) at the Air Host Inn motel on Virginia Avenue, near the airport. Captain Smith started the meeting with general information about the projected growth of the airline and then he made the announcement, "Gentlemen, Delta has hired its first black "stewardess" and the company expects you to treat her with the same degree of respect as the other "stewardesses". This news came as no surprise to the group since the rumors had already spread the information.

Despite the newly enacted Civil Rights Legislation, change was slow to come in some parts of the country. Blacks were not readily accepted by some employees or passengers in their new roles with the airlines. Previously, job opportunities for blacks were limited to Skycaps - the equivalent of railway porters who handled passengers' bags for tips. Some passengers refused to be served by a black "stewardess". Pat endured and went on to complete an exemplary 35-year career with Delta before retiring in 2001.

Whites Only

One hot summer day, in 1967, I was the copilot on a CV-440 flight to a small city east of Atlanta that was typical of some smaller cities in the South. The "stewardess" was a recently hired African American female. The CV-44 only had one "stewardess" to serve the 44 passengers. We had a two hour wait before the return flight to Atlanta and usually spent the time having lunch in the airport terminal restaurant. After all the passengers deplaned, I suggested to the captain that we ask our flight attendant to join us for lunch. He reminded me that the restaurant only served white customers and said, "I'll think of something".

The captain called the new flight attendant to the cockpit and told her that she was to be the "designated fire guard" while we were on the ground. She gave him a puzzled look and asked, "What are the duties of a fire guard"? "Didn't they explain that during your training", replied the captain. He continued, "The fire guard looks for evidence of smoke or fire in the cabin and is responsible for notifying the ground crew by running to the door and screaming "fire, fire"! I'm sure she knew this story was a lot of crap, but she just smiled and said, "You can depend on me". We went inside to have lunch and brought our flight attendant a box lunch. There was no ground air conditioning in those days, so when we got back on the airplane, she was soaking wet with perspiration. I never forgot this experience, but I'm sure it was just one of many such incidents for some of our early African American employees.

In 1968, Delta Air Lines hired its first African American pilot. Sam Graddy was a mild manner, soft spoken, Army pilot, who became legendary to many aspiring African American military pilots. Air Force pilot John Bailey remembers his call to Sam for advice. "Black pilots fly with white pilots every day, but they fly with a black pilot maybe once in a lifetime. It's up to you to establish a degree of comfort in the cockpit, so they're comfortable flying with you," John recalled. "Let them know that you're just another pilot." John Bailey was hired by Delta as a pilot several years later.

John and I spent one memorable winter flying together on a four-day trip that included a flight from Detroit to Portland, Maine with stops in Cleveland, Burlington, and Manchester. The next day we retraced the stops on the way back to Detroit. This was a real baptism for me as a new captain and John as a new copilot. I had never seen so much snow. As we approached Portland on one of these trips the weather was miserable – low, overcast skies, limited visibility with snow, and winds out of the north at 60 knots. This meant that we would have to land on RWY 36, which was only 5,000 feet in length. Any other runway would have exceeded our maximum crosswind component. The runway had been partially cleared by the snowplows, but the breaking condition was still only reported as "fair". John was flying the aircraft as we started the approach. The amount of turbulence was significant, but John kept the aircraft right on the ILS localizer and glide slope. Then he looked over and said, "Ron, let me know when you want the controls". I replied, "John, you've got all the experience you need for this approach and landing. It's your leg". John made a perfect landing and brought the DC-9 to a stop about half-way down the short runway. The wind had reduced our speed across the ground to around 60 knots at touchdown. As we exited the runway, John looked over with a big grin and said, "Wow"! We both laughed.

The same year that Sam Graddy started flying as a pilot for Delta, Cal Flanigan began his career as a mechanic with Delta. He had dreamed of flying ever since he was a boy growing up in Conyers, Georgia. After being drafted into the Army in 1969 for two years, Cal used the GI Bill and cash from his Delta salary to pay for pilot training at a time few other African American pilots were flying airliners. In 1976, he became a first officer flying the DC-9 for Delta. After 45 years of service, including 37 years as a pilot, Cal turned 65 — the mandatory retirement age for airline pilots. It is unlikely that Cal Flanigan's long tenure and attendance record would ever be replicated. During his career, Cal served as a Senior Flight Instructor, Line Check Airman and Delta's first African American International Chief Pilot in Atlanta — and he never took a sick day in 45 years.

Males Only

The late sixties and early seventies marked the end of the all-white flight attendant ranks and the all-white, all-male, cockpit crews. Connie Bowlin was a farm girl from North Carolina. She grew up with parents who believed in hard work and pursuing your dreams. Introduced to flying while in college, it was not until she met her husband that the opportunity to fly became a reality. Ed Bowlin was a Delta captain and with him as her husband, mentor, and offering encouragement, Connie realized her dream of becoming a pilot. While working as a Flight Attendant, she obtained her ratings from private to ATP and in March of 1978 she became the 4th female pilot hired by Delta - one of the first 50 women to be hired by a major carrier. Joy Walker, who was hired in 1973 became Delta's first female pilot. Connie was a Delta Air Lines pilot for 26 years and retired as a B-767 Captain. Connie holds numerous type ratings, including

Warbird aircraft such as the P-51 Mustang, B-17, C-47, and others. She and Ed flew their P-51 Mustang in many air shows around the country. They were inducted into the Georgia Aviation Hall of Fame in 2009.

Pilots Stephanie Johnson and Dawn Cook made history for Delta Air Lines in February of 2016. With Capt. Johnson and First Officer Cook at the helm of an Airbus A320 flying from Detroit to Las Vegas, the duo became the first African American women to make up the cockpit crew on one of Delta's "mainline" flights. As for Stephanie Johnson, she already had secured a Delta milestone by becoming the airline's first African American female captain.

Delta has become a very diverse company, flying to hundreds of destinations, in many different countries around the globe, with employees of just about every nationality, speaking many different languages - all working together for one common goal of providing good service to the customers. CEO Ed Bastian once summed it up by saying, "For more than 85 years, Delta has been in the business of bringing people together. As a global airline, we believe that our company must reflect the diversity of the world and serve as a model of inclusiveness. That commitment to embracing diverse people, styles, and ways of thinking, and treating our customers and each other with respect, is part of our core values. A global marketplace requires an innovative, inclusive workforce for business growth. By seeking diversity, promoting inclusion, and driving accountability, Delta can make a positive impact on its people, customers and the communities it serves."

Chapter 9
"There's Gold in Them Thar Hills"

This was the phrase yelled from the steps of the Lumpkin County Courthouse in 1849 by the Assayer of the Dahlonega Mint, Dr. M. F. Stephenson, to stop the exodus of miners from Dahlonega in Georgia to California, which had just started its own gold rush.

The World Headquarters for Delta Air Lines is in Atlanta. One of the most recognizable features of the Atlanta skyline is Georgia's gold-domed State Capitol. The gold for the dome was donated by the citizens of Dahlonega and Lumpkin County, the site of the nation's first gold rush in 1828. On August 4, 1958, a caravan of seven mule-drawn covered wagons left Dahlonega to bring the gold to Atlanta. Thereafter, the gold was sent to Philadelphia, where it was milled into gold leaf 1/5,000th of an inch thick, or about the thickness of a piece of tinfoil used to wrap chewing gum.

Georgia Belle

Like many airlines based in the United States, Delta was an early buyer of the B-747. Delta's first B-747 was delivered to Atlanta on October 2, 1970. At a special dedication ceremony, Governor Lester G. Maddox christened it the "Georgia Belle," sprinkling gold dust over the plane's nose from Georgia's Dahlonega mines. Recalling that Dahlonega, a city in the north Georgia mountains, was the site of America's first gold rush, Maddox added, "All the gold mined in Dahlonega could never total in value the amount of goodwill this airplane can deliver".

Delta used its B-747 fleet between the major cities of its route system, including Atlanta, Chicago, Dallas/Ft. Worth, Detroit, Los Angeles, Miami, New York, and San Francisco. It was the first Delta plane with a personal audio system for passengers, offering seven "Deltasonic" channels playing the Beatles, Bert Bacharach, and Beethoven.

The good times did not last for Delta and its B-747, however. The airline decided in 1974 that the jets were too big and began trading them back to Boeing. The "Queen of the Skies" was all but gone from the Delta fleet by April 1977, the jet's role largely taken over by the Lockheed L-1011 TriStar.

That would have probably been the end of Delta's history with the B-747 had it not been for the airline's merger with Northwest Airlines, which closed in 2008. With that, Delta welcomed the B-747 back into its fold. With Northwest, Delta acquired 16 passenger B-747-400s, two passenger B-747-200s (used for charter), and 12 B-747-200 freighters. Delta retired the B-747-200 passenger fleet in September of 2009. The smaller freighter fleet wasn't far behind, retiring in late December of 2009. Delta's passenger B-747-400 fleet held on strong, lasting for almost another decade. The jets operated mainly overseas flights out of Delta's Atlanta and Detroit hubs.

The B-747 Experience

On April 30, 2016, ship 6301, the first B-767-400 built by the Boeing Aircraft Company for Northwest Airline, moved to the Delta Flight Museum in Atlanta. After almost a year of work, this famous B-747-400 opened as an exhibition. Inside, visitors can sit in aircraft seats, check out the upper deck, walk out on a wing, examine what goes on behind the walls of an aircraft, and learn all about the history of the 747. Delta flew its final remaining B-747 to an Arizona scrapyard on January 3, 2018.

As for the State Capitol Dome, by 1977, only nineteen years after its application, almost half of the gold was gone from the dome. The gold was applied during the winter months, and the engineers were unaware that gold leaf does not bond properly when it is applied during cold weather. Concern over the disappearing gold and the dome's appearance led a few Georgians and state officials to explore how the dome might be regilded. The Dahlonega–Lumpkin County Jaycees committed their organization to raising the gold for the project, as they had done in the late 1950s, with overall responsibility for regilding to be assumed by the Georgia Building Authority.

The fund-raising effort was ambitious; a wagon train crossed the state, visiting each of the state's former capitals. In June 1979, after a journey of almost six weeks, the wagon train pulled up to the city limits of Dahlonega, where Governor George Busbee boarded the lead wagon and drove it for the final few miles.

Before the end of the year, enough gold for the dome had been collected.

By 1981 the total regilding of the capitol dome was complete. Gold leaf is very thin and vulnerable to heat, wind, and rain damage, so by the 1990s flaking was again occurring on the dome. Today, rather than waiting until the damage is visible from the ground, the Georgia Building Authority now repairs the damage as it occurs.

Don't You Like Amsterdam

Many years later, after I retired from Delta. The B-747 neared the end of her career, I learned that Delta was pulling all the B-747s out of Europe. She would spend her final days with Delta flying to Asia out of Detroit. I called a friend of mine, who was a retired Delta meteorologist, and asked if he wanted to fly to Amsterdam and back. He said, "Sure, who's going and how long is the trip". I explained, "It is just you and me. We're going to fly over and then jump on the next plane back to Atlanta. The whole purpose of the trip is just to fly the B-747 one last time before she retires".

We boarded the aircraft and took our seats in Delta One (first class) using employee space available passes. We enjoyed every moment of the flight. As we deplaned in Amsterdam, I went up to a KLM agent in the jetway and told her that we were making a connection and asked if we needed to go through passport control or could we go directly to the gate of the outbound flight. She asked where we were going. I replied, "Atlanta". With a puzzled look, she said, "This flight just came from Atlanta". I smiled and said," Yes, I know, we just got off this flight". Even more puzzled, the agent asked, "Don't you like Amsterdam". I couldn't help but laugh. Then, I went on to explain that we were employees and just wanted to ride the B-747 one last time before it retired. She gave us a big smile and directed us to the outbound gate.

On the ride home I got the last seat in Delta One. Conrad was not so lucky! He was stuck in a center seat in coach.

Information for this chapter was obtained from articles published in the Atlanta Constitution newspaper. The newspaper information was gathered from the Newspaper.com website.

Chapter 10
Who Doesn't Remember Mario?

I crossed paths with many wonderful people from all walks of like during my career with Delta and still have fond memories of some of the most colorful characters.

Delta Family Breakfast

Jean was a waitress at the airport Holiday Inn motel in Shreveport, Louisiana. The small motel was just across the street from a honky-tonk called the Westwood Club. There were no windows in the Westwood and the lights were always dim. Songs by country stars like Johnny Cash, Willie Nelson, and Waylon Jennings were always playing on the jukebox. The Westwood was a real joint, but it was the closest place to grab a quick hamburger after a long duty day with lots of stops and a short layover.

There was usually a good crowd in the motel dining room for breakfast each morning. Several flights had an early morning departure. Delta pioneered the "Early Birds"! Jean was a grandmother-like figure that loved the Delta pilots and flight attendants. She got up at the crack of dawn each morning and came to the motel to prepare "home-made" biscuits, so her "Delta Family" could start the day with a good breakfast. She had never been on an airplane, so the flight attendants decided to take up money to purchase Jane a ticket to Atlanta and give her a tour of the Delta General Office. After the tour, a Delta captain offered to take Jean for a ride in his open-cockpit Stearman.

The Stearman, Model 75, was a biplane formerly used as a military trainer aircraft. There were 10,626 of these built in the United States during the 1930s and 1940s. After WWII, thousands of surplus aircraft were sold on the civilian market, where they became popular as crop dusters, sport planes, and for aerobatics and wing walking use in air shows. I can just picture this sweet little lady sitting in the rear seat of the Stearman, with the wind blowing through her hair, and a big smile on her face. She must have been in hog-heaven!

The City of Angels

Another favorite place for breakfast was the second-floor restaurant in the Huntley House Hotel in Santa Monica, California. Jane and Jose took good care of the Delta crews and their three-egg omelet with fresh salsa and sourdough toast was the best.

Flight attendants swore the hotel had ghosts and told lots of stories about things going "bump in the night". I personally never saw a ghost in my hotel room!

In the late sixties, there was a small alley behind the Huntley House with some older apartments occupied by a group of hippies and next door was the Mucky Duck British Tavern, complete with dart board. Down the street was the open-air Santa Monica Mall. The pedestrian mall, built on what was Third Street, was home to Al Hirt's Java Club – another favorite for airline crews. The mall went through some hard times in the eighties, but it has now been renovated and is called the

Third Street Promenade. The Santa Monica pier always provided some great sightseeing of those "Itsy Bitsy, Teenie Weenie, Yellow Polkadot, Bikinis".

There are certain events in history that everyone remembers exactly where they were and what they were doing at the time. When President Kennedy was assassinated on November 22, 1963, I was in the yard, raking leaves, at our house on Old Colony Road, in East Point, Georgia and my wife was in the den ironing clothes. She ran to the door and screamed, "the President has been shot"!

I landed in Los Angeles (LAX) on July 20, 1969, the day Neil Armstrong became the first person to step onto the lunar surface. This was another one of those events that everyone remembers where they were at the time. I was in the limo riding to the hotel in Santa Monica and listening to the reports on the radio when I heard the famous words, "That's one small step for man, one giant leap for mankind." Horns started honking and people were hanging out their car windows waving in excitement.

The Hurcky Bird

Back in the late sixties and early seventies, laying over in San Francisco was like being on another planet: Cable Cars, Height-Ashbury Hippies, Scoma's at Fisherman's Wharf, Buena Vista Café Irish Coffee, China Town, Carol Doda's Peppermint Lounge, and the Topless Shoeshine Girls on Broadway Street.

Within a few months of graduating from initial training with Delta, I made the transition to Second

Officer on the Lockheed L-100 "Hercules" and headed back to school again for a Tubro-Prop Flight Engineer Certificate. This aircraft was the civilian variant of the C-130 Hercules military transport made by the Lockheed Corporation in Marietta, Georgia. With this plane, Delta offered the first single-carrier cargo service between California and the Southeast, filling a big gap between the aerospace industries in those regions. Our payload often consisted of parts for the automobile or aerospace industry, but we also carried everything from horses to dolphins in their large tanks of water. Delta operated this aircraft from 1966 until 1973. When Delta's widebody passenger jets—the Boeing 747, Douglas DC-10, Lockheed L-1011—arrived with their speed and large underfloor "belly bin" capacity, Delta did not need a fleet of specialized cargo aircraft any longer.

I flew the L-100 on a route from Atlanta to San Francisco with stops in New Orleans, Dallas, and Los Angeles. We normally flew at a cruise altitude of around 24,000 feet. One spring afternoon, the "jet stream" over the western part of the United States was lower than normal. The west to east winds at 24,000 feet were around 200 miles per hour. This would drastically reduce our ground speed between Dallas and Los Angeles. In those days, all jet airplanes had to operate under Instrument Flight Rules (IFR) and normally cruised at an altitude above 18,000 feet. However, the L-100, being a Turbo-Prop" could still operate under Visual Flight Rules (VFR) and not have to follow a prescribed route.

After taking off from Dallas, the winds aloft forecast proved correct. The headwinds became stronger the higher we climbed. The captain decided to cancel our IFR clearance and descended the L-100 to within 1500 feet of the desert floor to avoid the strong headwinds. We maintained this altitude all the way to Los Angeles. What magnificent sights as we flew low over the Painted Desert in Arizona and then swung north and flew along the North Rim of the Grand Canyon. This was a rare experience for a large transport aircraft. Something I will never forget!

The Canterbury

No trip down memory lane would be complete without including the world's most famous Filipino bartender, who worked at the Canterbury Hotel in San Francisco. When I first started flying to SFO on the L-100, crews stayed at the Sheraton Palace Hotel on Market Street. After we were moved to the Canterbury Hotel, Mario quickly became a great friend to Delta crew members. Everyone remembers his sense of humor and corny jokes. Several times each night, he would ring a bell and say, "Okay folks, drink up, you're wasting my time". Whenever an unfamiliar face walked in the door of the bar, Mario's favorite line was "Excuse me, sir, the gay bar is down the street".

Flying the B-747 into SFO was a big deal! Mario reserved a special table in the Canterbury bar, next to the popcorn machine, for the "jumbo jet" crew. There was always a generous supply of "hot sauce" for the popcorn, which was one of Mario's specialties. I had never heard of putting "hot sauce" on popcorn, but it wasn't too bad. Other crew members were not allowed to sit at the special B-747 table. A chair for the captain was at the head of the table. One of the" jumbo jet" captains, suggested to Delta that B-747 Captains should have a 5th gold stripe added to their uniform. Not!

Mario was one of the highlights of a San Francisco layover for years. Then suddenly, he was gone. I heard that he went back to the Philippines, but I never knew why. San Francisco was my all-time favorite layover on this side of the Atlantic.

Chapter 11
Underneath Gate 61

The hub of activity in Atlanta for Delta Air Lines during the sixties and seventies was the area underneath gate 61 on the F concourse of the Atlanta Jet Age Terminal.

Atlanta's modern jet-age terminal opened on May 3, 1961. The complex was the first in the world to be built specifically for jet aircraft. At the time, it was the largest passenger terminal in the country, covering sixty acres, with nearly a mile of concourses and 48 gates with parking for 52 aircraft. The enormous light-filled lobby and modern architecture was a far cry from the cramped and dreary temporary terminal that preceded it. In 1968, Delta doubled their number of gates by adding the rotundas to the ends of the existing concourses E and F. Despite the enormous size of the enlarged terminal facilities, it reached its design capacity shortly after opening and had become hopelessly overcrowded by the late 1970s.

The office that coordinated all of Delta's ground operations in Atlanta was located underneath gate 61. The Flight Plan, Dispatch Release, and Weight and Balance data for each flight was calculated by this office. The weight of the aircraft, fuel, cargo, and passengers were added together to obtain the takeoff weight of each flight. This information was used by the flight crew to determine the speed required for takeoff. Weather reports and forecast information were posted on a counter for the flight crew members. Flight dispatchers were available to discuss the weather or other dispatch matters with the captain of each flight.

The office was located between the pilot and flight attendant rest areas which consisted of rows and rows of black leather recliners. Crew members would sign in for their flight, seek out the other crew members to introduce themselves, and then catch up on the latest rumors or joke. In between flights this area provided a place to chit-chat and to get to know your fellow workers. Many lifelong friendships were developed in the crew rest area. Each group had a crew scheduling office at either end of the hallway.

The pilot schedulers sat behind a long counter that contained the monthly time sheets for each pilot and a place for them to sign-in for their flight. If a crewmember were late to sign-in, one of the schedulers would be on the phone looking for a replacement pilot that was on standby reserve for just such a situation. I only lived about 10 minutes from the airport, so I received a call quite often.

As you entered the door to operations the smell of leather filled the room. There were metal racks for the pilots' black leather flight kits, but as Delta rapidly expanded these racks were always full. Flight kits were sitting all around the room. It was hard enough trying to remember where you put it after the last flight, but then the cleaning crew would move them around at night so they could mop the floor. It would sometimes take forever to find your flight kit. Most pilots, even long after retirement, have dreams about delaying the flight while looking for their flight kit. A crew delay was a no, no! I've been retired for almost 23 years and still have this dream. Where the hell is the darn thing!

Just across the concourse from gate 61 was gate 62, which was located across the parking ramp from the airport postal facility. Many times, to avoid a flight delay, the instructions from a scheduler was to "get here as soon as you can and park at the post office, I'll move your car to the employee parking lot". There were times when I was sitting in the cockpit only 30 minutes after receiving the frantic call from crew scheduling.

Gate 62 was located next to the roadway leading to the terminal building, so a tight turn was required by aircraft parking at the gate. This did not present a problem until we got the DC8-61. The first few times the "stretched eight" parked at this gate the baggage bin doors would not open. The aircraft was so long that a binding moment in the fuselage would keep the bin doors from opening unless the aircraft was taxied straight ahead for a short distance. In addition, it was discovered that jet blast from the engines was blowing carts of mail into the post office. After that, the procedures required that the aircraft stop short of the gate and be towed-in by tractors.

The Post Office parking area was also used by Delta employees on payday. Back in those days, before direct deposit, paychecks came in an orange envelope and they were distributed by crew scheduling. Generally, a designee from each neighborhood would drive to the airport to pick up paychecks for all their friends. The

Post Office was the most convenient short-term parking.

By the 1970s, aircraft parking became so over-crowded that Delta and Eastern both resorted to using remote satellite aircraft parking. Eastern used "mobile lounges" that resembled a cross between a jetway and a bus on scissor lifts. These had been pioneered in the 1960s at Washington's Dulles Airport. Delta operated a fleet of buses that ran between the "remote pad" and Gate 61. Next to the stairs leading down to operations was a shoeshine stand in the concourse. I can still hear, "Shine 'em up, Delta fly girls!" coming from the shine stand.

Mid-Field Terminal

On September 21, 1980, Atlanta's enormous new passenger terminal, the largest in the world, opened for business. Dubbed "Midfield" because of its central location between the runways, the complex is still in operation today, although it has been expanded many times through the years. The pilots, flight attendants, and crew scheduling facilities were located underneath gate A19 in the new terminal for several years.

The dispatchers were moved to new facilities in the general office and were no longer available for a face to face chat with the flight crew. The crew scheduling office was the next to go. It also moved to the general office complex. The once familiar face of a crew scheduler simply became a voice on the phone to many new hire pilots. They would never get to know schedulers like Fred Smith, Wiley Pardon, and Doris Davidson, who finally retired from Delta after 55 years of service. It was a sad day. I became good friends with many of the crew schedulers and remain so today. The flight attendants were eventually moved to another area underneath gate A17. This was another sad day! We lost a lot of the camaraderie that made working for Delta so special. I am so thankful for the friendships developed underneath gate 61.

Chapter 12
Airport Historical Street Names

It is obvious how some of the streets around the Atlanta Airport got their names: Jet Road, Field Place, Crosswind Road, and Delta Boulevard. And, of course, Woolman Boulevard was named after the founder of Delta Air Lines, but who were some of the other people for which streets around the Atlanta airport were named? I drove these streets for years and never gave a thought as to their namesake. After some research, I found that many of them were pioneers in Atlanta aviation.

Doug Davis Drive

Douglas Henry Davis (1899 – 1934) was an early American aviator, barnstormer, air racer, flight instructor and commercial pilot. Born in Zebulon, Georgia, he was raised on a farm and attended Griffin High School. When the United States entered World War I in 1917, Davis left school in his senior year and enlisted in the United States Army Air Service. He graduated at the top of his class and was commissioned a second lieutenant, but, to his disappointment, was made an instructor, flying a Curtiss JN-4D "Jenny" trainer rather than fighting the enemy in the skies over France.

After his discharge in 1919, Davis purchased a surplus government Jenny, which he named "Glenna Mae" after his future wife and turned to barnstorming in the southeastern United States. He formed the Doug Davis

Flying Circus, and through the early 1920s, his barnstorming outfit competed fiercely with the rival Mabel Cody Flying Circus. Eventually the two merged and formed the Baby Ruth Flying Circus in 1924, after acquiring a sponsor in Otto Schnering, founder of the Curtiss Candy Company, which manufactured the Baby Ruth candy bar.

Doug Davis built the first permanent aircraft hangar at Atlanta's Candler Field Airport in 1927. In 1930, he joined Eastern Air Transport (the predecessor of Eastern Air Lines) and piloted the first commercial airline flight from Atlanta to New York City. Davis died while competing in the National Air Races on Labor Day of 1934. Leading on the eighth lap, he missed a pylon, banked to turn around, and try to pass the pylon properly, only to stall and crash into the ground, dying instantly out of sight of the 60,000 spectators. The announcer lied and told the crowd he had bailed out.

His son, Doug Davis Jr., was six at the time of his father's death. He would become a successful painter before dying in the Air France B-707 crash on takeoff from Orly Field, Paris, in June of 1962, at about the same age as his father.

Perry J Hudson Parkway

Perry Hudson (1916 – 1998) was a Major in the US Army Air Corps during WWII and Chief Pilot for Eastern Airlines. He served 8 years as a State Senator and 12 years as the Mayor of Hapeville. He is buried in the College Park Cemetery off Virginia Avenue.

Perry's son, Jack Hudson (1942 – 2002) was a pilot for Delta Air Lines from 1970 until his death in 2002, from complications following a massive heart attack. He attended Hapeville's College Street School and graduated from the Hapeville High School in 1960 where he was captain of the football team and served as senior class president. Jack graduated from the United States Air Force Academy in 1964 and served in Southeast Asia flying with an air search and rescue unit. He was awarded the Air Force Cross, the nation's second highest award for valor, for combat action which resulted in the successful rescue of fifty-four US troops. Before leaving the war zone, Captain Hudson was himself shot down, but escaped injury and was quickly retrieved by his fellow flyers.

Toffie Terrace

Affectionately known as Toffie, Harold William Tofflemire (1897 – 1983) was born in Pipestone, Minnesota. He moved south and started working for Eastern Airlines at the Daytona Beach Airport in 1930. Tofflemire served as the Station Manager in Jacksonville, Miami, and New Orleans before becoming the Station Manager in Atlanta. The last eight years before retirement he was the Southeast Regional Director of Stations for Eastern Airlines with 20 stations under his authority. His office was in a small red brick building that was located where the Delta, Atlanta North Hangar is now sitting. This maintenance hangar was originally built by Eastern and acquired by Delta some years later.

In the 1950s, Atlanta's Municipal Airport was Eastern's busiest hub, thanks to its central location on the route map. In 1955, Delta Air Lines pioneered the hub and spoke system at its Atlanta hub to compete with Eastern. A fierce rivalry developed, and each airline pumped millions of dollars and thousands of jobs into Atlanta's economy. They helped propel the post-World War II city into its unchallenged place as the capital of the modern South.

I first met Toffie in 1961, after graduation from high school, while applying for a job as a part-time gate agent. This launched my career in aviation. Customer Service employees with Eastern, at the time, started out working 20 hours per week, in 4-hour shifts. The Atlanta airport had several pushes throughout the day when every gate was filled and some gates had airplanes double parked, but in between pushes the airport was quiet. Utilizing employees in 4-hour shifts made the most efficient use of manpower. The Atlanta airport was the busiest airport in the United States in 1957 with two million passengers passing through, and it was the busiest in the world between noon and 2:00 PM each day.

By 1966, I had acquired the necessary training and begin seeking employment as an airline pilot. Toffie arranged for me to fly to Miami and be interviewed for a pilot position with Eastern, but it was not to be.

In his obituary, the Atlanta Constitution newspaper notes that Mr. Tofflemire, of College Park, Ga., was known as "Mr. Eastern Airlines" in Atlanta. He was the first person to be inducted into the Eastern Airlines Hall of Fame. Toffie was president of the Airport Area Kiwanis Club, the East Point Chamber of Commerce, and the Draper Boys Club in College Park. In 1970, The Moose Club named him "Mr. East Point". For ten years, he served as chairman of the South Fulton Area Cancer Drive, six years as the chairman of the South Fulton Community Chest Drive, and eight years as Chairman of the March of Dimes Drive. Toffie also chaired the initial fund-raising drive for the South Fulton Hospital.

Candler Way

Asa Griggs Candler (1851 – 1929) was an American business tycoon who in 1888 purchased the Coca-Cola recipe for $1,750 from chemist John Stith Pemberton in Atlanta, Georgia. Candler founded The Coca-Cola Company in 1892 and developed it as a major company. Prominent among civic leaders of Atlanta, Candler was elected and served as the 41st Mayor of the city, from 1916 to 1919.

Candler Field, the site of the present-day Hartsfield-Jackson Atlanta International Airport, was named after him, as is Candler Park in Atlanta. Candler and two associates purchased acreage on the south side of Atlanta to be developed into a lavish racetrack modeled after the Indianapolis Speedway. The racetrack opened in 1909, but poor revenue forced the raceway to close after one season. The former speedway was used to host aerial exhibitions consisting of endurance flights, and over the years the property was used for various aviation events.

In 1925, a permanent airfield was needed, and several civic organizations were looking for a suitable site. Asa

Candler offered up his former speedway to lease to the city for five years if they city would pay the taxes. Atlanta Mayor Bill Hartsfield proposed they name the new airport Candler Field in hopes that Asa Candler might eventually donate the land to the city. On April 13, 1929, Candler sold the airport to the city of Atlanta for $94,400.

In 2005, retired Delta captain, Ron Alexander bought a small airport south of Atlanta that was originally called "Antique Acres" when it was started in 1967 by Carl Hoffman, another Delta pilot. Ron was a visionary who had big plans for turning what was then called Peach State Airport into a vintage aerodrome reminiscent of the original Atlanta airport, Candler Field, as it existed in the 1920's and 1930's. He built the vintage-style American Airways hangar, established Candler Field Museum, and moved Barnstormer's Grill & Event Center to its current location next to the museum in 2008. Tragically, in 2016, Ron, and his passenger, an FAA official, were killed in a Curtiss JN-4 Jenny bi-plane crash near his Peach State Airport in Williamson, Georgia.

In the spring of 2018, Keven and Linda Sasser purchased Peach State Aerodrome and Barnstormer's Grill from the Alexander family. Keven was a friend of Ron and the two spent many hours together discussing Ron's dreams and plans for the airport and restaurant. In 2019, the museum closed its memorabilia displays to the public with the goal of building a new 7,700 sq. ft. facility that will serve as a permanent home to its aviation artifacts as well as to the growing Youth Aviation Program.

Hartsfield Drive

William Berry Hartsfield, Sr. (1890 – 1971) was an American politician who served as the 49th and 51st Mayor of Atlanta, Georgia. His tenure extended from 1937 to 1941 and again from 1942 to 1962, making him the longest-serving mayor of his native Atlanta, Georgia. Hartsfield is credited with developing Atlanta's airport into a national aviation center. The Hartsfield-Jackson Atlanta International Airport is named in Hartsfield's honor as well as a later mayor, Maynard Jackson, who led the modernization of the airport in the 1970s. Hartsfield was responsible for fostering Atlanta's image as "the city too busy to hate" during the civil rights struggles of the 1950s. In 1957, he won election to his last term as mayor by defeating the staunch segregationist and future Governor Lester Maddox.

Information about people named in this chapter was obtained from articles published in the Atlanta Constitution newspaper. The newspaper information was gathered from the Newspaper.com website.

Chapter 13
Fly Delta Big Jets

Prior to 1959, all Delta aircraft were piston-engine powered, but, in 1959 Delta began the transition to jets. The company entered the jet age when it secured early DC-8 delivery positions from Douglas Aircraft.

The 14th DC-8 off the assembly line was Delta's N801E, Ship 801, named "Pride of Delta." On delivery day, July 22, 1959, Ship 801 flew the 2,497-mile route from the Douglas plant in Long Beach, California, to Miami in 4 hours and 43 minutes.

Delta raced to install Atlanta airport's first passenger boarding bridge, called a "jetway," just in time for the arrival of the first DC-8 flight. Ship 801 flew the world's first DC-8 passenger service. Delta Flight 823 departed New York International Airport (Idlewild) for Atlanta at 9:20 am, on September 18, 1959. The inaugural crew consisted of Captain Floyd Addison, First Officer Jack McMahan, Second Officer Hank Freese and Flight Attendants Jeanette Easley, Beverly Comerford, Elizabeth Whitman, and Carolyn Jones.

Delta Ship Numbers 801 – 806 delivered as DC-8-11, then upgraded to DC-8-12, and later to DC-8-51 standard. In March of 1962, a Delta DC-8 is the first airplane to fly between Los Angeles and Atlanta in less than three hours. The official time was 2 hours, 57 minutes, 11 seconds. Ship 801 was the star performer in scientific coverage of the solar eclipse on July 20, 1963. Equipped with spectrographs, special cameras, telescopes and other astronomical instruments, Ship 801 carried some 60 scientists, including astronaut Scott Carpenter, on a 520-mile chase of the eclipse across the Canadian Northwest. The mission was sponsored by Douglas Aircraft Company and National Geographic Society.

In 1967, Delta took delivery of the DC-8-61 (Stretched Eight). It was 37 feet longer than the standard DC-8. It offered 60% more seat capacity than the standard DC-8, yet the operating costs were no more than 10% higher. The long cabin could accommodate 252 seats in an all-economy layout, but Delta's two-class configuration held 195 passenger seats.

Hijackings

Aircraft technology was rapidly changing the way we flew, but these were incredibly stressful times for the airline industry. The number of aircraft hijackings was alarming. Captain Bill May was in command of Delta Flight 841 from Detroit to Miami when it was hijacked by members of the Black Liberation Army in July of 1972. Five hijackers, who had boarded with three children, took over the aircraft using weapons smuggled on board, including a handgun hidden inside a bible with its pages cut out to form a cavity. The aircraft flew to Miami as originally scheduled, where 86 passenger hostages were released. It was then flown to Boston, where the aircraft was refueled, and the required international charts were brought on-board, along with a navigator for the overseas portion of the flight to Algiers, Algeria.

Delta didn't fly any overseas routes at the time. Maintenance foreman Ronald Fudge refueled the plane and delivered the navigator to the plane along with a bag containing the $1 million dollar ransom (in $50 and $100 bills). He also brought bags containing provisions requested by the hijackers, including cigarettes, apples, and ham and cheese sandwiches. It was the most money ever paid for the release of airplane hostages. Upon arrival in Algeria, authorities seized the aircraft and ransom, which were returned to the U.S. The hijackers were released after a few days. Four of the five hijackers were captured in Paris in 1976 and tried by the French courts. After forty years on the run, the remaining hijacker, who had dressed as a priest during the hijacking, was arrested in 2011. The long arm of the law found the hijacker living in Sintra, Portugal.

In 1974, at the Baltimore/Washington International Airport, a hijacker shot and killed a Maryland Police Officer before storming Delta Air Lines Flight 523, which was still sitting at the gate preparing for the 7:00 am departure for ATL. When informed by Captain Doug Loftin and First Officer Fred Jones they could not take off until wheel blocks were removed, the hijacker fired a warning shot and grabbed a nearby passenger, ordering her to "fly the plane." As he reentered the cockpit, he shot both pilots. The hijacker was mortally wounded when a county police officer stormed the plane and fired four shots through the aircraft door with a .357 Magnum revolver. Two of the shots penetrated the thick window of the aircraft door and wounded the hijacker, who then committed suicide by shooting himself in the head. First

Officer Jones died as he was being removed from the aircraft. The motive was to hijack the aircraft and crash it into the White House, in an assassination attempt on President Richard Nixon.

After the first hijacking of a U.S. airliner in May of 1961, President John F. Kennedy assembled the first group of 18 sky marshals and assigned them to the FBI. Between 1968 and 1972 there were 75 U.S. flights hijacked to Cuba, mainly by exiles and extortionists. In 1970, U.S. Customs Service established a greatly expanded sky marshal program with 1,784 agents. In 1974, the Federal Aviation Administration took over the air marshal program and reduced their ranks as X-ray screening begin at U.S. airports. Despite the airport screenings, hijackings continued well into the 1980s.

Other Delta flights hijacked to Cuba included: Flight 1061 from New York (LaGuardia) to Fort Lauderdale in June of 1979; an L-1011 flight from San Juan to Los Angeles in August of 1980; a New Orleans to Atlanta flight in September of 1980; Flight 722 from Miami to Tampa in July of 1983; Flight 784 from Miami to Tampa in August of 1983; and Flight 357 from New Orleans to Dallas in March of 1984. Thankfully, nobody else was injured in any of these other hijackings.

A list containing the most notable aircraft hijackings from 1910 through 2010 was compiled by Wikipedia and published on the internet website.

The Lockheed Tristar

The L-1011 (Tristar) made its appearance in 1973. The crew consisted of 3 pilots and 10 flight attendants. I was in the first class of pilots trained to fly the aircraft as a First Officer. The "high, wide and handsome" cabin provided extra space throughout the interior. It had seats for 250 passengers (50 First Class, 200 Economy). Three double-width entry doors on each side of fuselage and wider aisles allowed easier, faster boarding and deplaning.

Meals were served from a lower-deck galley – the only one in aviation history. Two elevators provided access to the main cabin. It was the first U.S. commercial jetliner able to land with a zero-foot ceiling (height of clouds) and with a 700-foot RVR (runway visual range). This meant fewer diversions from inclement weather. The "New Advanced Automated Navigation System" featured a tv screen that operated like a moving map which navigated the airplane between cities. It connected to the Auto Pilot and Automatic Landing System, giving truly automatic flight. She was a marvelous airplane. Way ahead of her time! Delta flew a total of 70 L-1011s, up to 56 at one time—the largest L-1011 fleet in the airline industry.

Chapter 14
The Saving of Delta Flight 1080

It was nearly midnight at the San Diego airport as the Delta Air Lines jet accelerates down the runway, bound for Los Angeles in April of 1977.

When it hits 126 knots, the plane unexpectedly noses up before the pilot pulls on the control column for takeoff. Speeding into the heavy clouds over the ocean, the nose pitches even higher. The amazed pilot desperately slams the control column forward as far as possible to try to force the nose back down.

This was the beginning of one of the most harrowing 55 minutes in aviation history. The passengers were lucky enough to have Captain Jack McMahan at the controls. A burly, 56-year-old, he was one of Delta's most experienced captains. During 36 years of flying, he piloted biplanes, Grumman Wildcats (as a Marine Corps pilot during World War II) and over a dozen passenger planes, including all models of jumbo jet. There were eight stewardesses on board, and in the cockpit were Wilbur Radford, the copilot, and Steven Heidt, the engineer.

As Captain McMahan shoved the control column forward in response to the too-steep climb, the plane's nose came down slightly and, at least momentarily, the plane seemed to return to a normal climb. At an altitude of 400 feet, however, the plane began nosing up again. The electric trim, didn't seem to work, so he tried "manual trim." That didn't work either. There just wasn't any response. He tried both again, with no effect.

At 800 feet, with the plane climbing into thick clouds, Jack asked the engineer, to check the hydraulic system through which most of the controls work. He unlatched and reset all switches associated with the plane's trim, or angle of flight. The copilot checked control-panel warning lights to make sure they were working properly. By 3,000 feet altitude, all emergency procedures concerning pitch and trim had been tried, and the crew couldn't find out what was wrong.

Air-traffic control was notified of the plane's plight by radio. Both the captain and the copilot got on the controls, exerting full forward force on the control column. Even so, as the plane climbed out over the Pacific Ocean, it pitched up more and more, far above the normal 15 degrees. As the pitch attitude increased, the speed was rapidly decaying, 150 knots...145....140. In that sequence, the plane was fast running into the danger of a fatal stall. The air moving across the wing wasn't providing enough lift. The solution for that problem is to get the nose down and increase air speed, but the crew just couldn't get the nose down.

We're Number Three

Suddenly, Captain McMahan had the horrifying realization that he was going to lose it. He had a clear mental picture of exactly what the aircraft was going to do - stall, roll to the left and descend vertically, disappearing into the clouds - at night - into the water. A week before, a Southern Airways DC9 had crashed, killing 68. And the week before that the Pan Am and the KLM planes had collided on Tenerife. Accidents come in threes, they say, and McMahan thought, "My God, we're number three."

At that instant, the captain yanked all the throttles back, reducing power. For a pilot, it was an unnatural and illogical move. Reducing power would cut air speed further, and that would seem to increase the risk of a stall. But, at this stage, you quit being methodical - you just do something and do it fast.

The tactic worked. There was a little change in control feel, a little more control over the plane. Captain McMahan, then advanced the No. 2 throttle, which increased the thrust of the No. 2 engine in the tail of the L-1011. On the L-1011, the two engines hanging on the wings of the plane, Nos. 1 and 3, are canted slightly downward, and their thrust makes the plane pitch up. But the No. 2 engine in the tail is canted slightly upward, and its thrust makes the plane pitch slightly downward. The increased thrust applied to the No. 2 engine did exactly that.

The nose slowly began to come down, to about 18 degrees; speed began picking up, to about 150 knots, and at 9,000 feet the plane broke out of the overcast and into the bright moonlight. By adjusting the throttles slightly, the captain was able to stabilize the plane at about 10,000 feet.

Jane Hooper, the flight-attendant coordinator, had sensed something was wrong and went to the cockpit. She was told there was a control problem and was asked to move all the passengers forward in the cabin to help get the nose down. It probably didn't help much, but in that situation, every little bit would help. Then she was told to go back and "strap herself in".

What Now

The question was, where to land? The captain immediately ruled out returning to cloud-covered San Diego. Palmdale Airport and Edwards Air Force Base were considered, but they close at 10 p.m., and it was after midnight. Phoenix and Las Vegas also were considered, but those choices would mean flying over the Sierra Nevada, where turbulence could be fatal to a plane already hard to control. That left Los Angeles International. Despite cloudy conditions there too, Los Angeles was chosen.

Which direction should the plane come in from? The captain was offered the option of flying over Los Angeles itself into the airport, but he could imagine the holocaust if the aircraft went down over the city. McMahan figured if he was going to lose it, he should lose it over water. So, the Delta flight would come in from the ocean. That had some disadvantages. Pilots dislike landing over water at night because there aren't any visual reference points. Among pilots, it's called landing "over a black hole." But that approach also held advantages: it made possible a long, straight-in approach. It would give the crew plenty of time to stabilize the plane and handle any control problems.

A normal touchdown, however, would be impossible. With no control over pitch so the pilot could force the nose down on the runway, the plane might float across the airport on a cushion of air and crash at the end. Even worse, as it neared touchdown, it might suddenly pitch up a couple of hundred feet, stall, then crash down into the runway. With no altitude to maneuver, there would be nothing the pilot could do.

The solution, Captain McMahan figured, was to come in with flaps on the wings set at a reduced angle. That would allow the plane to come in at a higher speed - 170 knots instead of a normal 130 - which was risky itself, but it would allow the pilot to "bang" the plane down on the runway. What he wanted was that positive ground contact. The final seconds would be the key.

The approach descent began, and the Delta jet coasted down into the clouds hanging over Los Angeles. The copilot radioed to the Los Angeles tower to have fire trucks stand by. He also gave the number of passengers, so that enough ambulances could be called.

Then, at 2,500 feet, the landing gear was extended, shifting the center of gravity, and the plane abruptly pitched up again. The captain shoved the control column full forward, but the aircraft continued to climb while air speed deteriorated. It was going above the landing glide slope. His first thought was: Since we can't control the aircraft with the landing gear down, retract the gear, turn south and ditch in the ocean parallel to the coast. Instead, he again boosted power on the No. 2 engine and cut thrust on No. 1 and No. 3. Slowly, slowly, the nose began dropping.

Copilot Radford: "1,000 feet - everything looking good - on glide path, on course."

At 500 feet, the Delta jet breaks out of the clouds, and the runway is dead ahead.

Captain McMahan: "I'm gonna touch down and get on the brakes. . . right down the middle . . and get it on . . Help me hold the controls. . ."

The plane slams onto the runway at 170 knots, and as Captain McMahan applies brakes, the copilot calls out the speed. Copilot Radford: "130 . . . 120 . . . 110 . . . 100 . . . 90 . . . 80 . . . 70 knots, 60 knots, thank God."

Engineer Heidt: "Wheeee-eh." Tower: "Well, Delta 1080, everything okay?"

True Hero

Captain McMahan: "Tell'em we're all right - we'll take it to the gate." Jane Hooper rushed into the cockpit and kissed the pilot. "What was the problem?" she asked. Engineer Heidt answered, "We had up, but no down; we just kept going up, and up and up." What had gone wrong? Within hours Lockheed and FAA engineers were swarming over the plane. The stabilizer has, on its trailing edges, small "elevators" that flip up and down in conjunction with the movement of the stabilizer, and the engineers quickly found the left elevator had stuck in the up position, causing the plane to pitch up. (There isn't any warning light in the L-1011 cockpit to indicate a malfunctioning elevator because the stabilizer is the main controlling device. In the dark night, there wasn't any way to see the jammed elevator, even if the problem had been suspected. Hence, there wasn't any way for the pilot to figure out what was wrong.

Why had it stuck? Water from rain, fog and mist had dripped down a structure in the tail onto a bearing. As the plane had repeatedly ascended and descended during the many flights, changes in pressure had sucked the water into the bearing. The bearing corroded and broke. When Captain McMahan maneuvered his flight controls just before takeoff, the elevator, linked to the broken bearing, jammed.

As for Delta's crew and passengers, they switched to another Delta plane and took off for Dallas, the next stop for Flight 1080. On the way to Dallas, Captain McMahan got a note from a passenger saying, "All that screwing around in L.A. is going to make me late for a connection - what are you going to do about it?" "The best he could", was the reply.

Captain McMahan won the FAA's prestigious Distinguished Service Award for bringing Flight 1080 in safely. Will Radford and Steve Heidt received FAA certificates of commendation.

The Saving of Delta Flight 1080 is still one of the most miraculous events in aviation history and Captain Jack McMahan was a true hero.

Very few people knew the story about Delta flight 1080 until they read about it the Washington Post. The newspaper interviewed Captain McMahan, after he won the Distinguished Service Award from the FAA in 1978 and wrote about the details of the flight. The account of the incident was taken from the interview and newspaper articles.

Chapter 15
The Delta Prince

In the sixties and seventies Delta was rapidly expanding, so I transitioned from airplane to airplane almost every year: DC-6 & DC-7, L-100, CV-440, DC-9, DC-8 and the Lockheed L-1011.

In 1976, I made the transition to captain on the DC-9 – the Delta Prince as it was called. It was back to east coast flying for the next ten years. I really loved flying the DC-9 into some of the smaller cities around the country. The small crew-size made for a close-knit group. During my first month as a captain on the DC-9, the copilot and I took our sons along with us on a trip to Charleston, South Carolina. At the time, Delta would not provide the crew with a hotel unless the "lay over" was longer than 8 hours. The crew would try to grab a few hours shut eye in a black chair in the employee break area before the early morning return flight to Atlanta.

As we taxied toward the ramp, the tower controller asked if he could bring his son down for a tour of the airplane. He too had brought his son to work. I said, "Sure, if you will give our sons a tour of the tower"! After the tours, we all went to breakfast together. I let our sons ride on the cockpit jump seat, which was not exactly according to company policy. While the passengers were deplaning in ATL, one of them said with a smile, "Did the boys enjoyed riding the jump seat". I expected a call from the chief pilot, but the call never came. Thank goodness! Yep, the good old days!

Red Carpet Tour

In April of 1982, I was fortunate enough to be selected as captain of the Red Carpet Tour, the first year it was flown by Delta Air Lines. I asked First Officer Don Hubbard to serve as my copilot and flight attendants Grace Nicholson, Susan Powell, Sally Gregringer, and Debby Curry were all handpicked by the Inflight Service department. Harold Bevis, Director of Public Affairs, was part of the entourage representing Delta and the State of Georgia. Previously the charter had been flown by Southern Air Lines, but Delta was awarded the contract starting in 1982, and still operates the charter flight today. Don and I flew the charter for several more years before I moved up to captain on the B-767.

The Red Carpet Tour is a premier 4-day annual event, held each April, by the Georgia Chamber of Commerce and the Georgia Department of Economic Development. It provides an opportunity for important business leaders from around the world to attend The Masters, and to learn more about doing business in the State of Georgia. Since its inception, the event has been responsible for bringing billions of dollars of industries to Georgia. A second location, that differs from year-to-year, provides further exploration of the state. Other cities visited have included Albany, Athens, Atlanta, Columbus, Dalton, Gainesville, Rome, Savannah, and Valdosta.

We flew to Augusta on Thursday, the first day of tournament play, and then returned on Saturday.

Passengers deplaned in Augusta and were bussed to a VIP hospitality tent at the golf course. After repositioning the aircraft to a remote area of the airport, the crew members changed clothes and were driven to the golf course by the Georgia State Patrol, with "blue lights" flashing. We felt like celebrities as the patrol cars pulled up to the VIP tent. We all got VIP badges that would allow us access to anywhere on the grounds – except the inside of the clubhouse!

Flight Over Sapelo

George Busbee, who was the first Georgia governor to serve two consecutive four-year terms (1975-83), after a revision of the state constitution, was along on the first Red Carpet Tour flown by Delta. We spent two full days at The Masters and a day of sightseeing in Savanah, Georgia. Gov. Busbee had a pilot's license and loved to fly, so he asked to sit on the cockpit jump seat for the entire 3 days instead of taking his seat in First Class. Early on Saturday morning, as we taxied out for takeoff in Savanah, the governor had a special request. I called the tower and asked for a VFR (Visual Flight Rules) departure, followed by a low flight along the coast, and over Sapelo Island, before picking up an IFR (Instrument Flight Rules) clearance to Augusta. This was a very unusual request and there was complete silence on the radio, so I explained that it was the desired of the Governor, who was sitting on my jump seat. The tower quickly replied, "Roger, cleared as requested". As we flew down the Georgia coastline at 1,000 feet AGL, the governor was on the PA describing the scenery and giving passengers information about the state-owned barrier islands. With our sightseeing tour complete, we climbed the DC-9 to cruising altitude and headed back to The Masters for another ride in the State Patrol cars.

Moving On

Craig Stadler was the 1982 Masters Champion, by winning the shortest playoff in Masters history. After retiring from office in 1983, Governor Busbee became a partner in the prestigious law firm of King & Spalding and served on several corporate boards, including Delta Air Lines. Several years later, Don was diagnosed with cancer and died. Harold was promoted to Vice President of Public Affairs. George Busbee suffered a massive heart attack at the Savanah Airport and died in 2004. At the request of the tour participants and tour organizers, Grace, Susan, and Debbie continued flying the Red Carpet Tour for another twenty-something years.

In recent years, Delta has staffed the charter flight with crew members on reserve status instead of using a hand-picked crew. I'm quite sure the crew members flying the charter today continue to provide a great level of Delta service, but the camaraderie is no longer part of the tour. The annual reunion and the bonds of friendship that were developed over the years with corporate giants, from all around the world, their host dignitaries from the State of Georgia, and the Delta crew members that flew the tour, finally came to an end. Those involved will never forget the experience of flying on the Red Carpet Tour and the friendships that developed.

Chapter 16
It Never Rains in the Desert

In the spring of 1982, over 7,000 employees, friends, and the international media gathered at Delta's Technical Operations Center to present the airline with its first Boeing 767, Ship 102, christened "The Spirit of Delta." It was purchased with voluntary contributions from employees after Delta experienced their first quarterly loss in the company's history. The aircraft flew as an ambassador of Delta pride and culture for over 23 years. Painted in special liveries to celebrate the 1996 Atlanta Olympics and Delta's 75th Anniversary in 2004, she retired on February 12, 2006, after flying 70,697 hours and 34,389 trip cycles. Repainted in its original 1982 Delta livery, "The Spirit of Delta" took off on a two-week cross-country, 12-stop Farewell Tour. Delta employees, friends and charities shared in Spirit's final flying days from February 21-March 6, 2006. She now sits proudly in the Delta Flight Museum in Atlanta.

In 1986, I made the leap from the DC-9 to the left seat of the B-767 and was as honored to be able to fly the "Spirit of Delta"! That summer, I was flying a trip that had a long layover in Las Vegas and my teenage son, Jeff, was in high school and had just taken up playing golf. I thought it would be fun to take him along with me on the flight and spend some time bonding on the Desert Inn golf course. It was just down the Strip from the Dunes Hotel where the Delta crews stayed.

When Delta first started flying to Las Vegas in 1961, the crew members stayed at the famous Sahara Hotel. In the early days, hotels in Las Vegas were eager for the airline business to help fill the empty rooms. As the popularity of the casinos grew, the hotels used the rooms to attract high-rollers and no longer wanted the airline business. By the mid-eighties, Delta crews were staying at the Dunes Hotel on the opposite end of the Strip.

Tournament of Champions

The Desert Inn Golf Club opened in 1952. Since its beginning, golf's greatest players, from Jack Nicklaus and Arnold Palmer, to Greg Norman and Tiger Woods have played golf on these infamous fairways. It was the only golf layout on the strip and its fairways were located just outside the Desert Inn Hotel and Casino. The original performance venue at the Desert Inn was the Painted Desert Room, later the Crystal Room, which opened in 1950 with 450 seats. Frank Sinatra made his Las Vegas debut there in 1951 and became a regular performer. The 18-hole golf course hosted the PGA Tour Tournament of Champions from 1953 to 1966.

The Dunes, themed after the Arabian Nights stories, opened in May of 1955. The hotel's slogan was "The Miracle in the Desert". From the time of its opening, the Dunes was known for the 35 ft tall fiberglass sultan statue that stood above its main entrance. Although it opened to much fanfare, it struggled from the start because The Dunes was at the then-southernmost part of the Strip. The hotel frequently had to borrow money to survive. To attract customers, the hotel brought in famous celebrities and entertainers such as Frank Sinatra, who dressed as a sultan. The Dunes was demolished in 1993 with a grand ceremony that involved major fireworks displays and the use of several "cannon blasts" from the English ship 'HMS Britannia' of Treasure Island Hotel and Casino. Over 200,000 people watched its demise.

As I descended the B-767 into the McCarran Airport in Las Vegas, we finally broke out of a solid overcast that covered the city. The weather radar didn't show any rain showers in the area, but the grayish sky wasn't too promising for a round of golf. The hotel was a short distance from the airport. Jeff and I quickly changed clothes and headed to the golf course. I think the green fee was around $125 per person, which was considerably more than I anticipated. Concerned about the threatening skies, I asked the attendant about the refund policy in the event of rain. He said," Sir, it never rains in the desert! After you hit the first ball you have played the course, there is no refund policy." We headed for the first tee and began to enjoy the experience of playing golf on this famous course. I think it was on the fourth hole that it started raining cats and dogs. It was miserable! We were soaking wet! Jeff said, "Dad, let's go back to the hotel". I replied, "Didn't you hear the man? It never rains in the desert! We're going to finish this round". Thankfully, the rain soon stopped, and we played the remaining 14 holes.

Hops In The Hanger

Some thirty-five years later, in 2019, I took Jeff and grandsons, Zac, Taylor, and Bo to the "Hops In The Hanger" party at the Delta Flight Museum. Two of my best friends from high school and their sons came along. Don Stevens was also a pilot for Delta and Sonny Smithwick was a Safety Inspector for the FAA. It was such a fun evening!

As we walked through the museum, looking at the beautifully restored airplanes and sipping craft beers, I was telling stories about the good old days in aviation. As we toured the "Spirit of Delta", sitting proudly in hanger number two, I was telling everyone the story about the employees donating money to purchase this B-767 airplane, Ship 102, for Delta Air Lines in December of 1982. Jeff spoke up and said, "Dad, you didn't tell them the most important story about this airplane." I gave him a puzzled look. He continued, "The "Spirit of Delta" was the airplane you flew to Las Vegas when I was in high school and we played golf at the Desert Inn." He was right! It was Ship 102 that carried us to Las Vegas that day.

Chapter 17
Transatlantic

In April of 1978 Delta was awarded a route from Atlanta to London, Gatwick (LGW) its first transatlantic flight. Authorization for flights to Frankfurt (FRA) followed in June of 1979 and service to Paris, Orly (ORY) started in April of 1985.

Before construction of the Charles de Gaulle International Airport (CDG) in 1974, the main airport of Paris was Orly (ORY). Even with the shift of most international traffic to the new airport, ORY remained the busiest French airport for domestic traffic, and the second busiest French airport overall in terms of passenger boarding's. More than 33 million passengers used the airport in 2018. When Orly first began operating in 1932, it went by the name of Villeneuve Orly Airport. Located on the outskirts of Paris, it was conveniently sited close to the city center.

During the Battle of France, in May of 1940, Germany invaded the Low Countries, and France. In just over six weeks, German armed forces overran Belgium and the Netherlands, captured Paris, and forced the surrender of the French government. As a result, Orly Airport was used by the occupying German Luftwaffe as a combat airfield, stationing various fighter and bomber units at the airport throughout the occupation. Consequently, the airport was repeatedly attacked by the Royal Air Force, and United States Army Air Forces (USAAF), destroying much of its infrastructure, and leaving its runways with numerous bomb craters to limit its usefulness to the Germans.

After the Battle of Normandy, and the retreat of German forces from Paris in August of 1944, Orly was partially repaired by the United States Army Air Forces, who was the primary operator at the airfield until March 1947, when control was returned to the French Government. By 1948, Orly was once again serving Paris with an increasing number of airline flights. Charter flights in the early 1960s were extremely popular, and Air France featured a fleet of regular Boeing jet planes that carried more than three million passengers each year.

High Museum of Art

Air France Flight 007 crashed on June 3, 1962, while on take-off from Orly Airport. Air France had just opened its new office in downtown Atlanta, and this was the inaugural flight. It was filled with many of Atlanta's elite citizens. The Atlanta Art Association had sponsored a month-long tour of the art treasures of Europe, and 106 of the passengers were art patrons heading home to Atlanta on this charter flight.

According to witnesses, during the takeoff roll on runway 8, the nose of Flight 007 lifted off the runway, but the main landing gear remained on the ground. The aircraft had already exceeded the maximum speed at which the takeoff could be safely aborted. However, the flight crew had no other choice, and attempted to abort the take off. With less than 3,000 feet of runway remaining, the pilots attempted to stop the B-707. They braked so hard, the main landing gear tires and wheels were destroyed, and caught fire. The aircraft ran off the end of the runway destroying the town of Villeneuve-le-Roi.

The only survivors of the disaster were two flight attendants seated in the back of the aircraft. The rest of the flight crew, and all 122 passengers on board the B-707 were killed. At the time, the crash was the worst single-aircraft disaster, and the first single civilian jet airliner disaster with more than 100 deaths. Later investigation found indications that a motor driving the elevator trim may have failed, leaving Captain Roland Hoche and First Officer Jacques Pitoiset unable to complete the rotation and liftoff.

The Woodruff Arts Center, originally called the Memorial Arts Center and one of the United States' largest, was founded in 1968 in memory of those who died in the crash. The loss to the city was a catalyst for the arts in Atlanta that helped create this memorial to the victims and led to the creation of the Atlanta Arts Alliance. The French government donated a Rodin sculpture, The Shade, to the High Museum of Art in memory of the victims of the crash.

Twin-Engine Transatlantic

During the first 10 years of Delta's transatlantic service, flights operated with Lockheed L-1011 aircraft. Starting in 1990 some of the European flights started using the B-767-300ER aircraft. This was the first twin-engine aircraft certified to fly transatlantic flights.

My first flight into Paris Orly was in early 1991 on a B-767-300ER. I had just completed the International Ground School portion of my training and was on my Transatlantic Operational Experience (TOE) flight with Line Check Airman (LCA) Ray Orrie. Pilots were required to make two international flights under the supervision of an LCA as part of their training.

As we approached Orly, early in the morning, we were instructed to enter a holding pattern to await a weather improvement. The airport was covered by dense fog, which was not forecast when we left Atlanta the night before. Rats! We didn't have an abundance of holding fuel! We began to prepare for a diversion to our alternate airport of Luxembourg (LUX). I had a gut feeling this was about to be an interesting experience. We notified Delta Flight Control in Atlanta of our diversion and learned that Lufthansa personnel in LUX would refuel our airplane for the flight back to Paris.

After landing in LUX, a "follow-me" truck escorted us to a remote parking place away from the terminal. A Lufthansa vehicle approached the aircraft, and I opened the cockpit sliding window to communicate with the driver. Captain Orrie and I climbed down the loading stand that was brought to the forward door and jumped on the Lufthansa baggage tug for a ride to the terminal. It took almost two hours to complete the refueling operation and get a new flight plan back to Paris. By the time we landed at Orly sometime after noon, the fog had cleared, and it was a beautiful day. The crew was exhausted by the time we got to the Le Meridien Hotel in the Montparnasse section of Paris. Welcome to international flying!

For me, foreign travel quickly became an obsession. Mark Twain said, "Travel is fatal to prejudice, bigotry, and narrow-mindedness, and many of our people need it sorely on these accounts. Broad, wholesome, charitable views of men and things cannot be acquired by vegetating in one little corner of the earth all one's lifetime." How true!

Check Point Charlie

Another memorable experience was my second TOE flight with Captain Herb Summers. It was the inaugural flight from Atlanta to Berlin. The Berlin Wall, which had encircled East Berlin for twenty-eight years was in the process of being demolished.

The crew hotel was in West Berlin, which looked like any other modern city in Germany. However, as we walked down Unter den Linden Street in East Berlin, we were amazed by the number of drab buildings that showed little sign of life. Bullet holes from WWII were still visible on many of the buildings.

Then we headed over to the Check Point Charlie museum, which is dedicated to showing how people attempted to escape East Berlin during the time it was under communist control. I brought home a small piece of the Berlin Wall that still sits in my office in a plastic case.

Information about the Air France crash was obtained from the Newspaper.com website.

Chapter 18
There'll Never Be Another Mainz

As I set in the classroom listening to lectures about international flying procedures, I kept thinking about the kid from southwest Atlanta, who traveled to the Great Smokey Mountains in Tennessee for vacation each year. He would soon be flying a B-767ER to London, Paris, Frankfurt, Munich, or other exciting places in Europe. It all seemed so unreal!

Terms like Nat Tracks, Coast-out, Coast-in, Plotting Charts, and Oceanic Clearance were becoming part of my vocabulary. I was amazed when the instructor told us that 800 flights per day operate on the North Atlantic Track System between the United States and Europe. Transatlantic flights usually make the eastbound crossing during the night and the westbound crossing during daylight hours. The "tracks" are not stationary routes shown on a map. The longitude and latitude of a track changes from day to day depending on the winds at altitude. The flight crewmember - usually the copilot - drew the assigned track on a blank Plotting Chart. This has most likely been discontinued with today's technology.

Radar tracking does not extend over the ocean, so aircraft are separated by altitude, time, and distance. The crew reports the aircraft position every 10 degrees of longitude and the controlling ATC agency uses this information to control the flow of traffic across the ocean. Airspace west of 30 degrees longitude is controlled by Gander Oceanic and airspace east of this line is controlled by Shanwick Oceanic.

Back in the nineties, the dominant means of long-distance communications with air traffic control was high frequency (HF) radios. Depending on atmospheric conditions, the reception was sometimes quite poor. Aircraft on the "tracks" monitor a common VHF frequency and rely on each other for turbulence reports and other information. If weather conditions were good, the channel was usually quiet. Occasionally, the silence would be broken by friendly chatter, but this practice was discouraged. If the chatter became too frequent, one of the Lufthansa pilots on the frequency would usually remind everyone "quite bitte, die Frequenz ist für business ".

The Frankfurt Hub

Even before the Pam Am acquisition in 1991, Delta already had established quite an operation in Frankfurt. We operated flights to Frankfurt from ATL, JFK, DFW, CVG, MCO, and SFO. The flight crew members stayed at a Hilton Hotel in the small city of Mainz, just across the Rhine River from the Frankfurt airport.

Crew members soon began to discover some of the great little restaurants in Mainz. Margo's, Sabina's, Helmut's, Wolfgang's, Doctor Flotte, and the Chicken House were some of the favorites. Of course, these were not the names of the restaurants. It was what they were called by the crew members, who couldn't pronounce the German names. The name usually referred to a favorite waitress or the owner of the restaurant. The

Chicken House was named for the wonderful roasted chicken they served. Yum, yum!

As we descended toward the Frankfurt airport, on my first international flight after training, I could see some of the small towns dotting the Rhine River - Bingen, Rudesheim, and Mainz. Beautiful! I had to pinch myself to make sure this was real. After landing, I started to taxi toward the terminal and missed turning onto the assigned taxiway. The controller asked in a gruff voice, "Is this your first time in Frankfurt". With a big smile, I thought about the response attributed to an old WWII, Delta Captain, several years earlier, when he was asked the same question. His reply, "Well, I was here during the war, but we didn't land". However, I thought otherwise about making a similar comment and simply acknowledge that it was my first time in Frankfurt.

As I boarded the crew-bus, I noticed a large cooler filled with German beer and a basket with one-dollar bills sitting near the door. Wow! What a great idea! A nice cold German beer for the ride to the hotel, after the long over-night flight. The bus drivers provided this service for several years before some teetotaler reported it and Delta ordered the practice stopped.

After the Pan Am acquisition in 1991, Delta operated something like 132 flights per day out of Frankfurt at its peak period. Each morning a caravan of 50-passenger buses transported the layover crews from the airport to the Mainz Hilton hotel. Each night, Delta crewmembers occupied most of the hotel's 431 rooms.

Our flight had a two-day layover in Frankfurt, so everyone was discussing their plans. Another captain on the bus found out it was my first international flight, so he suggested a river cruise. The river cruise boats docked right behind the Mainz Hilton hotel. The pilots offered to buy the White Wine and Champaign and the flight attendants agreed to supply the cheese, bread, and grapes. The next morning, we had "breakfast" while cruising down the Rhine River from Mainz to St. Goarshausen. Again, I had to pinch myself!

Ein Pils Bitte

The Hilton hotel in Mainz was filled with Delta crew members each night. Hans, the hotel manager, was a tall, lanky German without much sense of humor. The Bistro was a small restaurant owned by the hotel, but it didn't open until 7:00 or 8:00 each night, so most crew members went elsewhere for dinner. We usually gathered in the lobby around 5:00 pm to decide where to eat. A few of us started talking to Hans about opening the Bistro at 5:00 for happy hour, but he was not too keen on the idea. We assured him that we could fill the place each afternoon if he would just give it a try. So, a few weeks later the hotel announced that the Bistro would open at 5:00 pm and each crew member would be given a wooden token good for one free beer when signing into the hotel. By 4:30 people were already lining up outside the Bistro with token in hand. OMG, it was packed every night. Thanks, Hans!

Another character was Wolfgang. He owned a small restaurant near the BP gas station on Rheinstrasse, not far from the hotel. I think the DFW based flight attendants discovered this place. One Thanksgiving,

Wolfgang allowed the flight attendants to bring a turkey and all the trimmings to his restaurant and cook Thanksgiving Dinner for the entire crew. It soon became a favorite gathering place for crew members. The flight attendants left Jenga and several other games behind the bar for some after dinner entertainment. Wolfgang had a great collection of 50s and 60s rock and roll songs on his jukebox.

It was several years after my retirement before I got back to Mainz for the Christmas Markets. Wolfgang was still there, but most of the other Delta hangouts had changed ownership or gone out of business. The Chicken House has changed hands, but the new owner told me that he had heard many, many stories about the Delta crews from the previous owner. Margo's is now a fancy wine bar. Sabina, who worked at a restaurant near the City Hilton, married a DFW based Delta Captain, and they opened a restaurant everyone called the "Tree House". It had a large tree in the courtyard of the house where the restaurant was located. After the Captain retired from Delta, the restaurant was sold, and they moved to Spain. I heard recently that problems with the owner has caused them to move back to Mainz and reopen the "Tree House"!

Delta only has a few flights into Frankfurt these days, so I suspect things are rather quiet in Mainz. We had some great times during the good old days of the Frankfurt hub, but enough reminiscing. I was so fortunate to have been a part of this history.

Chapter 19
Home for the Holidays

In the song White Christmas, Bing Crosby says, "I'll be home for Christmas, if only in my dreams". Like most airline employees, I worked my share of holidays. However, I usually managed to be home for at least a portion of Christmas, when the kids were young. There were a few times when I had to fly over the entire Christmas holiday. One of the worst I can remember happened during my days as a copilot on the DC-9.

The Delta Prince, as the DC-9 was called when it was first introduced, was christened on October 7, 1966 by "Stewardess" Carol Koberlein, using a bottle containing water from twenty rivers in Delta's area of operations. Delta was the lead customer for the Douglas DC-9. Later that day, the airplane was flown to Atlanta by Delta's legendary Captain Thomas Prioleau Ball, the airline's Director of Flight Operations.

Christmas Cheeseburgers

A typical duty day on the DC-9 consisted of lots of stops, followed by a short layover in a small city, at a mediocre hotel. One Christmas Eve, we landed at Shreveport late in the afternoon and headed downtown to the hotel. I think the flight attendants stayed at a motel near the airport. The captain asked for a quiet room away from the elevators since we had an early morning departure. The desk clerk said we could have any room we wanted because we were the only two guests in the hotel. We had not eaten all day, so we were famished. The restaurant in the Greyhound Bus Terminal was the only place open, so we walked down the deserted street to the bus terminal for a quick cheeseburger before hitting the sack.

I woke up the next morning and looked at the clock, rubbing my eyes in disbelief. I didn't get my wake-up call and it was well past our pick-up time. I called the front desk, but nobody answered. I called the captain's room and woke him up. Neither one of us got a wake-up call. I threw on my uniform and headed downstairs, where I found the desk clerk sleeping on a sofa in the lobby and the limo driver was sound asleep in a chair. We woke the driver and headed to the airport for another long day. Merry Christmas!

The Rubber Chicken

During my early days as a DC-9 captain, I was scheduled to fly during Thanksgiving one year. My wife and I were shopping at a large mall when I happened to notice a novelty and magic store. I went in to browse. Sitting on the shelf was a skinned, rubber chicken. Hmmmm, this gave me an idea! I bought the chicken and took it along with me on the Thanksgiving trip to ORD. We had several stops along the way. I gave the chicken to the flight attendant, who put it on a platter and walked down the aisle asking the passengers, "What would you like for lunch". The passengers thought it was funny.

Then I had another brilliant idea. After landing at each stop, I would open the cockpit window and put the chicken under the windshield wiper. Bird strike! Each time we taxied into the ramp, the guys with the parking wands would spot the chicken and die laughing.

Everything was going great until the final stop in ORD. After landing, I put the chicken under the windshield wiper. As we approach the gate, the guy with the parking wands didn't notice the chicken until we were almost at the stopping point. Then it happened! He spotted the chicken and started laughing. He started shouting to others and pointing at the chicken.

We were moving very slowly anticipating a stop signal. The only problem, the guy with the wands was so distracted that he didn't give us the signal. The nose wheel "nudged" the chock and the airplane came to an abrupt stop. The flight attendant came to the cockpit and exclaimed, "What the hell happened?" The rubber chicken disappeared into my flight kit, never to be seen again.

Halloween in Brighton

In 1978, Delta began transatlantic service from Atlanta to London. The flight was required to use the smaller Gatwick airport, located about an hour's drive south of the city center.

For a time, crews were transported to a layover hotel near Hyde Park. However, the complaints begin to mount about the long ride in morning traffic, so the crews were moved to a hotel in the seaside, resort town of Brighton. It was a much shorter drive and the quaint little town quickly became a big hit with the crew members.

The hotel was located across the street from the pebble-covered beach and a short walk to the Brighton Palace Pier, with an amusement park like Santa Monica Pier in LA. Just behind the hotel was an area laid out according to a medieval street plan. "The Lanes", as it was called, was a maze of lanes, some covered, that formed a hidden nest of shops. A flight attendants dream! There were many good restaurants close to the hotel.

The strangest looking building in Brighton is the Royal Pavilion or Brighton Pavilion. Beginning in 1787, it was built in three stages as a seaside retreat for George, Prince of Wales, who became King George IV in 1820, after his father's death. The unique appearance of the Pavilion, with its Indo-Islamic exterior, was the work of architect John Nash, who extended the building starting in 1815.

One year in October, I was on L-1011 reserve and got a call from crew schedule. I was being assigned to the Atlanta - London flight over Halloween. I asked my wife, Carol, if she would like to come along and told her that we could attend a play at the nice little theater in Brighton. Little did I know what was in store!

Back then, the CVG based flight attendants organized a couple of events each year. The Mach Schnell (English: Make It Quick) Volleyball Tournament was held in Mainz during the summer and the Halloween Party in Brighton in the fall.

When I got to the airport, I learned that the original Captain was sick and couldn't take the flight. The rest of the crew told me about the Halloween party that was planned for Brighton and asked if I brought a costume. The answer was no since I had never heard anything about a Halloween party in Brighton. However, I was sure something would be available at one of the shops in "The Lanes".

The next day, I went shopping for a costume. That night, when I walked into the bar, I couldn't believe my eyes. There were clowns, go-go dancers, Mr. House-of-Cards, Mr. Budman, Cleopatra, and a copilot dressed in a traditional Nun Habit – complete with a white headdress that framed his face. The best costume belonged to Captain Howie Lynch, who was dressed in a red sequined evening gown, with large boobs, and a red wig.

After a few beers, I went to the men's room. The copilot with the Nun Habit was standing at a urinal with his skirt hiked up. About that time, an English chap walked into the bathroom. He took one look at the Nun and said, "Ops, sorry, I must be in the wrong room!" We died laughing! Another fun night in Brighton!

Thanksgiving in Dublin

The Burlington was the Delta layover hotel in Dublin for many years. Frequently the hotel manager, Mr. Doyle, greeted the crew bus and welcomed us to the hotel. He was always a perfect gentleman and looked exactly the way you would expect an Irishman to look – rosy cheeks and a red nose.

Each Thanksgiving, the hotel prepared a traditional Thanksgiving meal with all the trimmings for the crew members and their family. Most everyone usually brought along a spouse or another family member. Carol was along with me for this special event, that was hosted by Mr. Doyle in one of the private hotel dining rooms. I was lucky enough to fly this trip over Thanksgiving in 1996 - the year of the Summer Olympic Games in Atlanta. The return flight to Atlanta didn't operate on Thanksgiving Day, so we had a two-day layover.

At the beginning of the month, I suggested to the other members of the crew that we bring a little goodie-bag to Mr. Doyle to thank him for his generosity. Back in those days, pilots and flight attendants generally flew together for the entire month. We packed a shopping bag with some delicious southern goodies: peanut brittle, peach preserves, pralines, Jack Daniel's Whiskey, and I even bought an Atlanta Olympic ball cap with an Irish Flag on the side. We arrived in Dublin on Thanksgiving Eve morning. Mr. Doyle was there to welcome us and invited everyone to attend happy hour in the hotel bar later that afternoon - the tab was on him. How could we refuse?

The next day we went sightseeing and then stopped at O' Donoghue's pub for a pint before gathering at the hotel for our Thanksgiving meal. It was obvious from the decorations on the table that the Irish didn't know too much about how we Americans celebrate Thanksgiving. Each plate had a "New Year's Eve" hat, noise maker, streamers, and a small bag of confetti. Mr. Doyle made a few opening remarks, thanking Delta for using the Burlington, and wished us all a "Merry Thanksgiving". Then we dug into the scrumptious meal that tasted home cooked!

After dinner, I thanked Mr. Doyle and presented him with all the goodies. One by one, I told him a little about each product that was traditionally southern since this was Delta's heritage. That was my last layover at the Burlington. I'll never forget Mr. Doyle, and I'll never forget the Thanksgiving in Dublin.

Delta Dream Vacations

Holidays were quite a bit different flying the international circuit. The last year or two before retirement, I purposely bid for long layovers over a holiday to take advantage of as many "Delta Dream Vacations" as possible and took Carol along with me for most of these trips. One was a very memorable Christmas in Barcelona.

The flight was scheduled to leave Atlanta in the afternoon and make a stop in Madrid before continuing to Barcelona. It was the longest duty day of any of the international flights. Often, the flight was delayed leaving MAD because of ATC delays and would not arrive at BCN until almost noon. Barcelona was a great layover despite the endurance contest involved in just getting there.

The hotel on Avenida Diagonal was home for Delta crews for many years. El Corte Ingles, a large department store, was just down the street and there were a few good local restaurants nearby. Our favorite restaurant, Los Caracoles (The Snail) was located just off La Rambla, an interesting pedestrian street, just a short metro ride from the hotel. Two of my favorite dishes at Los Caracoles were their Paella and Garlic Chicken. I have been there several times since retirement.

Now for the Christmas story! On the first trip in December, we made a list of everyone on the crew that would be flying the trip over Christmas, so we could begin making plans. The flight attendants spent the entire month, bringing decorations and storing them in a closet at the hotel. We departed ATL on the 23rd of December and arrived in BCN on Christmas Eve morning. Everyone took a quick nap and then we begin preparations for a party in the suite provided by the hotel. Some people headed down to El Corte Ingles to purchase food and beverages, while others decorated the room. Most everyone on the crew brought a family member, so it was quite a large party.

On Christmas morning, we got up early and boarded a train to Monserrat, a rocky mountain range about an hour's journey from Barcelona. At the top of the rugged mountain is located the Basilica at Montserrat Monastery, where we attended the Christmas service. The world renowned Escolania Boys' Choir, consisting of 50 boys starting at age 10, would be performing during the service. Montserrat is home to one of the oldest boys' choirs in Europe. Documents testify to the existence of a religious and music school in Montserrat as far back as the 14th century.

After the service, we got a chance to see the main icon of the church - the Black Madonna. The statue of the Madonna and Child was believed to have been carved in Jerusalem at the beginning of the religion. Montserrat as a religious site traces back to the eighth century, when religious hermits lived there in caves. Legend says that the statue was hidden in a grotto in 718 to avoid it falling into the hands of Moorish invaders. The wooden statue has turned black with age. Her Spanish name is La Moreneta, which means "the black little one."

After the beautiful church service, we boarded a cable car for the ride down the mountain to catch the train back to Barcelona. During the train ride, we enjoyed a nice lunch consisting of Salami Sandwiches and Viento Rojo that we had purchased at El Corte Ingles the night before. This was my first visit to Montserrat, and it was the first time I had Salami Sandwiches and Spanish wine for Christmas dinner. It turned out to be a wonderful Christmas in Barcelona.

The Six Days of Christmas

Another memorable experience was a Christmas layover in Mainz, Germany. I was scheduled to fly into FRA on Christmas eve, fly to JFK on Christmas day, and then fly back to FRA the day after Christmas. Our kids were grown, so Carol accompanied me on the entire six-day trip. Many of the other crew members also brought a family member with them to Frankfurt. When we checked into the hotel, we were advised that most of the restaurants in town were closed on Christmas eve. A few of the crew favorites were open, but they were completely booked. I suggested that we meet at about

4:30 pm and go to Margo's before the crowds arrived to see if they could make room for us.

When I got to the lobby that afternoon, the front desk told me that Helmut had decided to open his Weisslilien restaurant and cook dinner for his Delta friends, but he would need some of us to help cook, tend bar, and serve, since his employees had the night off. We were the first crew members to arrive, so Helmut began to assign duties. Before long, the entire restaurant was packed with Delta people. I don't remember how long it took to serve everyone, but we were there for most of the night. It was the best Christmas dinner ever.

At the end of the evening, Helmut wished everyone a Merry Christmas and placed a basket beside the door for everyone to leave money for their meal. He had lost count of what everyone ate and drank. I hope everyone was generous! Unfortunately, Helmut was forced to close his restaurant several months later. Delta crew members lost a great friend!

On Christmas morning, we flew to New York. Our NAT TRACK from Frankfurt to New York carried us directly over Greenland. The weather could not have been better. From 35,000 feet it looked like you could almost reach down and touch the snow-covered peaks. The sun shining off the snow was almost blinding. Over the PA system, I invited the passengers to raise their window shades and look down at the magnificent sight below.

During the New York City layover, Carol and I attended the Christmas show at the Radio City Music

Hall, where her aunt worked as a Rockette for several years. The day after Christmas it was back to Mainz for a second round of Christmas cheer. That was certainly a Christmas to remember!

Chapter 20
That Night Over the Hindu Kush

When Delta inherited Pan Am's North Atlantic route system in 1991, it also gained a modest-size European hub in Frankfurt, Germany. Delta suddenly had fifth-freedom route access to a handful of new markets in Eastern Europe, all thanks to Pan Am's intra-European network from Frankfurt. Also included in the package were 5th-freedom rights to operate routes to Delhi and Mumbai, India 3-4 times per week.

Shortly after the acquisition, I was the captain of a Delta B-767 flight from Frankfurt to Delhi – a flight of some 3800 miles. The cockpit crew was based in Atlanta and the Indian flight attendants were all former Pan Am employees based in Bombay (Mumbai). Our flight departed in the afternoon and was scheduled to arrive in Delhi at around 2:00 in the morning.

The shortest distance between the two cities required flying over Iran, but no United States carrier had authority to fly this route. The first few flights to India operated on a southern route over the Middle East. Our flight was the first one to fly a shorter, more northerly route that carried us over Ukraine, the southern part of the Soviet Union, and a couple of the Soviet Republics in Central Asia. Most of the flight time was spent in territory controlled by the Soviet Union ATC. The official language of air traffic control world-wide is English, however, trying to communicate with the Russian Air Traffic Control was difficult at best.

After crossing over the Soviet Republics, our flight plan headed south over the Hindu Kush mountain range along the Afghanistan and Pakistan border before turning toward Indian airspace. The Hindu Kush is a formidable mountain range with most peaks being between 14,500 and 17,000 ft above sea level. The tallest peak rises 25,289 feet above sea level on the Pakistan side of the border.

Contact Kabul ATC

Sometime after midnight, we passed over Termez, Uzbekistan and the Russian controller handed us off to Kabul Air Traffic Control. Being unfamiliar with our "DL" call sign, the Kabul controller asked the nature of our flight. I explained that we were a scheduled passenger flight being operated by Delta Air Lines of the United States. He then asked for our "over-fly permit number". Some foreign countries require overflight permits to operate in their airspace and they charge the airline company a tax for the privilege of flying over their country. This information is usually transmitted to ATC along with the flight plan.

We instantly searched the flight folder and found permits for other countries, but nothing for Afghanistan. This was the first time in my career with Delta Air Lines that I was ever asked about an overfly permit. Meanwhile, we attempted HF radio communications with the Delta Flight Control in Atlanta, but HF radio reception was terrible that night and we were unable to establish contact with Atlanta. I explained to the Afghan controller that we were not aware Afghanistan required an over-flight permit.

At this point, the controller said that we did not have permission to proceed through Afghan airspace without a permit and demanded that we immediately reverse course. If we ignored the controllers demand, we would be flying through non-radar-controlled airspace without a clearance and would not know about other aircraft operating in the area. Considering the options, the decision was made to reverse course and return into Russian airspace until the situation was resolved. This presented another problem! We would be entering Soviet airspace without a clearance.

Pan Pan

The Afghanistan-Russian war had ended two years before, so we were not sure of just how much communication existed between controllers. We contacted the Russian controller, who was unaware of our situation. He became rather excited and started screaming into his microphone in Russian. The best we could determine, he was saying that we did not have permission to enter Russian airspace.

Over the radio, we declared the international distress call "Pan Pan", which means the flight has an emergency requiring some assistance or priority in handling, but the safety of the vessel or those aboard is not in immediate danger.

The situation was quickly going from bad to worse! We kept trying to explain that we were declaring an emergency and why we reentered Soviet airspace without a clearance. Suddenly a calm voice, speaking perfect English, came over the speaker. We explained the situation again and the controller cleared us to enter a holding pattern while he attempted contact with Kabul by telephone.

The co-pilot was finally able to make radio contact with Flight Control in Atlanta, who assured us that Afghanistan "did not" require over-fly permits. We told the dispatcher that our fuel condition would require diverting to an emergency airport if the situation was not soon resolved. We would not have enough fuel to continue to Delhi.

Operating over the mountainous region of the Hindu Kush required a special alternate that could be used in the event of an emergency. Our alternate this night was Tashkent, Uzbekistan. The only problem, the control tower and terminal building at the airport in Tashkent closed at midnight. The crew began discussing the gravity of the situation. We would be faced with landing at a mountainous, non-controlled airport, in the middle of the night, with 200 + passengers and crew sitting on an airplane at a deserted airport in Central Asia. Not a happy thought!

Sigh of Relief

After a few minutes, the Delta Flight Controller in Atlanta reported that they had found the over-fly permit and gave us the number – 30320-6001. We relayed this number to the Russian controller, who telephoned the information to the controller in Kabul. Permission was granted for us to proceed across Afghanistan for India.

After landing in Delhi, I headed straight to operations to telephone Delta Flight Control in Atlanta. I wanted to know why the over-fly permit information was not included in our flight folder. The dispatcher said, "To our knowledge, Afghanistan does not require an over-fly permit". So, I asked, "What was the number you gave me over the radio?" He explained that the decision was made to give the controller any number in hopes they would allow our flight to proceed. The number 30320-6001 was the "zip code" of the Delta General Office on Delta Boulevard in Atlanta"!

I'm sure there was a big sigh of relief in Flight Control when we reported that our flight was proceeding to India. There was certainly a big sigh of relief in the cockpit! The passengers were all sleeping, so they were never told about our situation. As we approached the airport in Delhi, we made an announcement apologizing for the delayed arrival due to stronger than normal headwinds.

To this day, I wonder about the Russian controller, who spoke perfect English. Also, I think about what would have happened if the Kabul controller refused to accept the number we provided. Future flights from Frankfurt to India returned to operating on southerly routes over Italy, Greece, Syria, the Persian Gulf, and the Arabian Sea until the situation with the overfly permits with Afghanistan was resolved.

In 1995, Delta service from Frankfurt to Delhi became contentious given tensions between the U.S. and the Persian Gulf countries, and with increased concerns over airspace security, the route was dropped.

Chapter 21
First Time in Moscow

Landing at the Sheremetyevo International Airport (SVO) in Moscow during the early nineties was like flying in a time warp. Originally built as a military airbase, Sheremetyevo was converted into a civilian airport in 1959. The terminal, later known as Sheremetyevo 1, was built in the early 1960s. It was the first airport in the Soviet Union that resembled a modern airport with check-in and departure areas as well as a cafe for passengers.

Opening in May of 1980 for the Moscow Summer Olympics, a new international terminal, Sheremetyevo 2, was built on the opposite side of the airport. The two terminals remained standing on opposite sides of the airport for almost 30 years. Making a flight connection from the domestic terminal to the international terminal was quite an ordeal.

In 1991, Delta had just acquired the European assets of Pan Am and it was my first time flying into Moscow. This was shortly before the collapse of the USSR and the economic crisis was causing panic among the population who were stuck with their increasingly worthless rubles. The official exchange rate of the ruble was 0.56 per dollar, but a single greenback sold for 30-33 rubles on the street. The Hammer & Sickle flag of the Soviet Union, flying over the Kremlin, was replaced with the flag of the Russian Federation on Christmas Day in 1991.

Uneventful Approach and Landing

Our flight attendants were former Pam Am, Russian speakers, who had flown into Moscow many times. Having this experience on-board gave me a sense of relief. I asked one of them to sit in the cockpit during the approach and landing in case we needed help understanding the Russian controllers. As it turned out, we didn't have much of a problem with communications. The approach and landing at SVO were uneventful. There was little air-traffic around the Moscow airport. The sky was clear, but I can't recall seeing much of the city. The visibility might have been limited by smog.

As we taxied to Sheremetyevo 2, I was amazed by the number of old, broken-down, military, and civilian aircraft parked all long the taxiways and terminal areas. It was like taxiing through one of the "aircraft graveyards" in the western deserts of the United States. Many of the planes had flat tires and were missing engines. I remember thinking, "this is the country that we feared for so long"!

Before passengers could deplane, a Soviet Passport Control Officer came aboard and collected the crewmember passports. We were told that the passports would be returned to us at the operations office. We deplaned and boarded a bus for the ride to operations, which was located underneath the terminal building about two gates away – walking on the ramp was not allowed. After a significant wait, one of our flight attendants had a few choice words "in Russian" and a "couple of bucks" for the Passport Control Officer. Our passports were promptly returned.

Red Square and Arbat Street

The crew hotel was in a park-like setting on a hill several miles from the city center. The copilots, and I were excited to be in Moscow for the first time and could not wait to grab a taxi to Red Square. The flight attendants suggested that we walk down to the main street and flag down a "street taxi" instead of getting one of the taxis in front of the hotel. Much cheaper! They also suggest that we go shopping on Arbat, the mile-long pedestrian street filled with vendors selling things from tabletops and small booths. Flight attendants always know the best places to shop!

We headed down to the lobby and asked the hotel Concierge for directions to the main street and asked him to write down the address of the hotel "in Russian" for the return trip. He graciously walked us out of the hotel, down the stairs, and hailed a taxi to take us to Red Square. More about this later!

After taking a few pictures of Saint Basil's Cathedral on Red Square and watching the changing of the guard at Lenin's Tomb, we headed over to Arbat Street for some souvenirs. The flight attendants told us the "best deals" could be obtained using American dollars, but you had to be careful since it was against the law.

I found a nice scarf for my wife and made an offer in dollars. The lady seemed extremely nervous about accepting American money, but she finally agreed. She told me to keep the money in my right hand and walk down the street. She would catch up with me and make the exchange. Sure enough, after walking about a block she came up beside me, slid a package under my arm, and took the money. I thought to myself, what cloak and dagger! As I continued down the street, I happen to look back just as two men in dark suits grabbed the lady by the arms and escorted her into an alley. I kept walking at a quick pace and did not look back again.

TrenMos

It was time to head back to the hotel, where we were to meet a person bringing some Black Lacquer Fairy-Tale Boxes to one of the flight attendant's room. He gave crewmembers a great price on these painted boxes that have been made in Russia for over two centuries. Each one depicts a fairy tale with a beautiful miniature painting. I had no idea what the boxes were all about, but the flight attendants insisted that I buy one for my wife. We bought some of the beautiful little boxes and then the entire crew headed over to TrenMos for dinner.

The Italian restaurant was a Soviet-American joint venture owned by the Public Catering Trust of Moscow's Lenin district, and a Ukrainian-American entrepreneur by the name of Shelly Ziger from Trenton, New Jersey – thus the name TrenMos. Ziger sent his 24-year-old son Jeff, a graduate of the Hyatt Hotel chain training course, to actively manage the restaurant.

As we stood on the sidewalk waiting for a taxi, one of the flight attendants spotted a large, white van coming down the street. She started waving her arms and the van pulled over and stopped. In Russian, she offered the driver two American dollars to give us a ride to the restaurant. He agreed! We jumped in and headed for TrenMos. Jeff loved chatting with the airline crews and provided endless bottles of Russian champagne from a large silver bowl in the center of the table.

Welcome to the Soviet Union

The next morning, I put on my uniform and headed down to the hotel restaurant for breakfast. I looked up and saw the hotel Concierge walking toward my table. He asked me to write a letter to the hotel manager explaining why he had left the hotel with me the night before. I said, "You just walked to the end of the building and showed us where to get a taxi"! He replied, "Can you please put that in the note to the manager"? I told him I would be happy to write the note, but I wondered why this was necessary. The Concierge said the hotel manager suspected that he was exchanging money for guests and cutting the hotel out of their commission. As I handed him the note, I made the comment "this is unbelievable". He replied, "No, this is the Soviet Union!"

When we got to the airplane, I notice two armed guards stationed at the front baggage-bin door and two armed guards stationed at the rear baggage-bin door. At the front of the aircraft was another uniformed guard. I was curious, so I went down to the guard at the nose of the airplane and asked him about the amount of security. He indicated that it was normal. I asked about his duties. He replied with a smile in broken English, "Watch the other guards". I gave him a set of the little plastic pilot wings that we hand out to the kids and he gave me a medal from the breast of his uniform in return. Nice exchange!

This was one of my few flights into Moscow before making the transition from the B-767 to the L-1011. Almost thirty years later, my Russian souvenirs still bring back fond memories of my first time in Moscow.

Chapter 22
As Heard from the Cockpit

Modern airplanes have tv screens located in the seatbacks showing movies and moving maps that display the aircrafts position, altitude, speed, and estimated time of arrival. On most flights today, the window shades remain closed for the entire flight and passengers remained glued to the screen. This is one of my pet peeves! I can't understand why people don't want to look out the window, even as the airplane is taking-off or landing. To me, it is still amazing to watch this giant- silver-bird take flight.

Back in the old days, passengers kept their window shades up the entire flight and looked at the beautiful world beneath them. Pilots had a list of PA announcements ready to describe some of the more prominent landmarks they were flying over. One clear day, a Delta jet was flying over Arizona. The copilot was providing his passengers with a running commentary about landmarks over the PA system. "Coming up on the right, you can see the Meteor Crater, which is a major tourist attraction in northern Arizona. It was formed about 50,000 years ago when a lump of nickel and iron, roughly 150 feet in diameter and weighing 300,000 tons, struck the earth at about 40,000 miles an hour, scattering white-hot debris for miles in every direction. The hole measures nearly a mile across and is 570 feet deep." From the cabin, a passenger was heard to exclaim," Wow! It just missed the highway!"

Reservations and Marketing

As the airlines begin putting jets into service, Delta's Marketing Department begin an advertising campaign to tell the public about the increased speed offered by the new jets. A man telephoned the reservations office in New York and asked, "How long does it take to fly to Boston?" The agent said, "Just a minute..." "Thank you," the man said and hung up.

Flying was quite expensive in those days, so the Marketing Department came up with a novel idea to attract new customers. They introduced a special half-fare rate for wives accompanying their husbands on business trips. Anticipating some valuable testimonials, the Publicity Department sent out letters to all the wives of businessmen who used the special rates, asking how they enjoyed their trip. Most of the responses were asking, "What Trip?"

This is Your Flight Attendant

It is rare to get a meal on a domestic flight anymore, but, in the old days, all coast to coast flights served a hot meal. You didn't have a choice of menu items in the coach section. Everyone ate the same thing. One of our flight attendants was asked by a passenger if he would like dinner. "What are my choices", he asked. "Yes or No," she replied.

Another flight attendant was on her first layover and was excited about the new experience. The next morning as the crew was getting into the limo, the captain noticed the new flight attendant was missing.

He knew which room she was in at the hotel and called her up wondering what happened to her. She answered the phone, sobbing, and said she couldn't get out of her room. "You can't get out of your room?" The captain asked, "Why not?" She replied, "There are only three doors in here," she cried, "one is the bathroom, one is the closet, and one has a sign on it that says, 'Do Not Disturb'!"

Air Traffic Control

Pilots and air traffic controllers can sometimes have disagreements about an instruction that has been issued. On a flight from New York to Los Angeles, the weather was causing departure delays. After a lengthy delay, the weather finally cleared, and the aircraft departed for LA. The captain decided he would try to make up the time lost by asking for a direct route. Halfway across the country, he was told to turn due south. Knowing that this turn would throw him even further behind schedule, he asked about the reason for the turn. The controller replied that the turn was for noise abatement. The pilot was infuriated and said to the controller, "How could I cause a noise problem when I am flying six miles above the earth?" The controller answered in a calm voice, "Captain, have you ever heard two 747's collide?"

Scary Experiences

People are always asking pilots if they ever had any scary experiences. Incidents do happen from time to time, but most pilots go their entire career without experiencing any real emergency. There are exceptions. The pilot of a DC-8 flight was approaching Atlanta when he discovered that the landing gear would not extend. It appeared the only option was to make a belly landing. The copilot called the ATL control tower and requested to have the landing runway foamed to lessen the chance of a fire. The captain instructed the flight attendants to have the passengers take their seats and get prepared for an emergency landing. A few minutes later, the co-pilot asked if everyone was buckled in and ready. "All set back here," came the reply, "except for the lawyers that are still going around passing out business cards."

Chapter 23
French Short Stories

I have experienced many interesting people and places during my travels around the world. Three of the most memorable stories occurred in France.

The French Resistance

In 2002, we were planning a two-week tour of France with another couple. My friend, Clay Wooten, was a change of life baby, and the youngest of nine siblings. He never knew much about his older brother, who died at age 21, during WWII. On the night of July 19, 1944, S/Sgt. Enoch Kalsie Wooten Jr. was the "top turret gunner" on a B-24, when his aircraft collided with a British Halifax, over the small French village of Marigny, south of Paris. The oldest member of the crew was the captain, 1st Lt. David Michlson, age 26. As part of the "Carpetbagger Mission", the US Army Airforce flight was transporting supplies to resistance groups operating in the enemy occupied western European nations. Both planes were to drop supplies to the French Resistance, but for some unknown reason they ended up in the same drop zone and had a midair collision at 1:00 o'clock in the morning.

The French Resistance was the collection of French movements that fought against the Nazi German occupation of France. Resistance cells were small groups of armed men and women who participated in guerrilla warfare activities, published underground newspapers, provided first-hand intelligence information, and maintained an escape network that helped Allied soldiers and airmen trapped behind enemy lines.

After the of death of S/Sgt Wooten, the family received a telegram from the government that mentioned the name of the little village where the crash occurred. Nobody in the family ever dreamed of going to France, so the name of the village was soon forgotten. After we started planning the tour, Clay found the telegram and his wife did an internet search for the village. She wrote a letter to the Mayor asking if anyone in the village remembered the incident and might know the location of the crash site. The Mayor responded with more information about the crash and suggested meeting Clay and Carolyn prior to beginning their tour of France.

The Mayor met them at the hotel Auberge De L'Atre in the nearby village of Quarre-les-Tomes and escorted them to Marigny. As they drove into the village, both sides of the street were lined with people waving American flags and throwing flowers at their car. A granite monument honoring the airmen has been erected in the village. My friends were completely overwhelmed by the reception. That night, they dined with the Mayor and some of the town's people at the hotel, where they were provided additional information about the crash. The next morning, they were taken to the crash site and presented with a few small pieces of metal that had been collected by the town's people from the wreckage. A bronze plaque marks the exact location of the crash site. The airmen from both airplanes were buried at the nearby Church of Marigny l'Eglise, and another granite memorial was erected in the cemetery in their honor. After returning to Paris, Clay and Carolyn told us the entire story - detail by detail – as the four of us cried.

Reliving D-Day
For the next two weeks we traveled around France enjoying the company of our young, female, French guide, Francoise, and learned lots of history. Near the end of the tour, our bus was pulling into the parking lot at Normandy and our guide made an announcement. "Ladies and Gentlemen, we will be getting off the bus soon and this will be my last commentary of the day". The passengers looked at each other in disbelief. Then she continued, "I will be turning the program over to one of your fellow passengers, who landed here on D-Day. He is going to share the experience with you today". We got off the bus and walked to a site overlooking the beach, where our fellow passenger described in detail what it was like on that fateful day in June of 1944, as a young 2nd Lieutenant landing in the first wave at Omaha Beach. There was not a dry eye in the group as he went through his story – minute by minute!

Monument to the Dead
In 2017, we made a port call in Brest, France on a cruise from Amsterdam to Athens, Greece. Located next to a sheltered bay, in the Brittany section of France, Brest is not far from the western tip of the peninsular. During

the Battle of France, Germany captured Brest and the harbor became a submarine base from which the German U-Boats attacked the Allied convoys operating in the North Atlantic.

During the war, Brest was attacked over 80 times by Allied bombers, but it would take until August 1944 before they succeeded in penetrating the bunkers with 9 direct hits from "Tallboy" bombs. The last U-boat left Brest on the 4th of September 1944 and on 21st of September the base was finally captured by the Americans, after a one-month siege and heavy losses. The harbor was heavily damaged by the Allied bombing raids and the city was destroyed, but it was completely rebuilt after the war ended. Located in the center of Brest is Place de la Liberte, the main city square, where the Monument to the Dead was erected in 1954.

As we stood in the middle of the square looking at a map of Brest, an old man with a walking cane approached us, speaking in French. He was looking at the map we were holding and pointed towards the harbor. Apparently, he thought we were lost tourists and was offering his help. With a smile, I said, "Sorry, English only"! Then he asked, "American"? When I replied, "Oui", the man pointed at the Monument of the Dead with his cane, placed his hand over his heart. Then he said, "Merci, Merci"! We just stood there for a few seconds, looking at each other, and our eyes filled with tears.

Chapter 24
Salty Dawg Saloon and the Travel Air

It was a beautiful summer day at the Salty Dawg Saloon in Homer, Alaska. The saloon, located at the end of the Homer Spit Road overlooking the Kachemak Bay, was filled with tourists mingling with fishermen and dining on fresh Halibut, while sipping lots of Homer Brewing Company beer. Homer is the Halibut fishing capital of the world. Paper money adorns the walls and ceiling of the saloon. Pinning paper money to the walls is a tradition that started years ago when fishermen pinned up notes as drink money for other fishermen still at sea. Life rings, some of which served as memorials to fishermen lost at sea, and other life rings for loved and respected fisherman, also adorn the walls.

The building, dating to 1909, was used as a post office, school, and for other purposes before the Salty Dawg Saloon officially opened in 1957. The building was moved to its present location on the Spit after the 1964 earthquake. The distinctive lighthouse was added to cover a water storage tank and has become one of Homer's more historical and recognizable landmarks. The lighthouse is reported to be the only navigational aid in the world located on top of a saloon. The Salty Dawg Saloon appeared in an episode of Discovery Channel's Deadliest Catch. It mentioned the bar's famous Duck Fart shot (layered Baileys Irish Cream, Kahlúa and Crown Royal whiskey).

In 1999, two years after I retired, we went to Alaska with another couple for a week or so of sightseeing before joining three other Delta couples for a cruise from Anchorage to Vancouver on the Sun Princess. Homer was the last stop on our itinerary before departing for the cruise. We left the Salty Dawg Saloon late in the afternoon and headed to our B&B for the last night in Homer.

Travel Air Flight

As we drove out of the Homer Spit, a sign along the side of the road advertising the Kachemak Bay Flying Service caught my attention - Antique Airplane Rides, 1929 Travel Air S-6000B. I just had to investigate! We turned off the highway onto Lambert Street and drove to the Kachemak Bay Flying Service docks on the shore of Beluga Lake.

I was disappointed to find the office had closed at 5:00 pm. With fewer beers at the Salty Dawg, we would have made it in time. Just as we were about to leave, the owner, Bill DeCreeft came out of the office. I told him that we really wanted to take a ride in his Travel Air, but we had to leave early the next morning. He said, "What do you know about a Travel Air"? I replied, "Well, I know it flew the first passenger flight for Delta Air Lines from Dallas, Texas to Jackson, Mississippi in 1929". He looked taken back and said, "Do you work for Delta"? When I replied that I retired from Delta as a pilot, he asked, "Do you know Captain Doug Rounds"? He went on to explain that Doug had assisted in the restoration of his Travel Air (NC9084), and then he brought out albums filled with pictures showing the restoration. The project included fitting the aircraft with floats to allow it to operate as a seaplane.

Delta Air Service launched its first airline service on June 17, 1929, with a Travel Air S-6000B, a high-wing, six-place, single-engine monoplane. Advertisements promoted the new plane as the "limousine of the air." Painted in sleek black and International Orange. The insulated, wood-paneled cabin featured woven wicker seats and hand holds rather than seat belts. Passengers could lower the roll-down windows for ventilation. It was designed to carry four passengers and two pilots, but because Delta flew with only one pilot, a fifth passenger could sit in the co-pilot seat. Delta's General Manager C.E. Woolman described its Travel Air amenities, as "accommodations for five passengers and pilot, toilet facilities, and space for hand luggage. Delta's restored Travel Air (NC8878) is one of the main exhibits at the Delta Flight Museum in Atlanta.

Bill DeCreeft first soloed in 1951 and started flying seaplanes commercially in 1961. He started Kachemak Bay Flying Service in 1967 and for the next 34 years flew sightseeing flights around Kachemak Bay, Cook Inlet, and the Kenai Peninsula, before retiring in 2001.

After we finished looking at his picture albums, I asked Bill if it might be possible to just go for a short ride to say that we had flown in the Travel Air, since we might never have the opportunity again. Anything, a take-off, circle the lake, and return for landing would suffice. Finally, Bill agreed. The cost would be $50 for a ride around the lake.

We eagerly jumped in the wicker-seats and beamed with delight as Bill taxied toward the end of the lake. As he turned the aircraft around and prepared for take-off, Bill looked over with a twinkle in his eye, "If you folks are not in any hurry, let's go for a real airplane ride".

We spent the next hour and a half flying over the Harding Ice Field and the glaciers of the Kenai Fjords National Park before returning to Homer. Then we flew over the Kachemak Bay and the Homer Spit before coming in for a landing on Lake Beluga.

Back in the office, I asked Bill how much we owed him for the fantastic experience. He looked at his wife Barbara, and with a smile said, "A deal is a deal, you owe me fifty bucks". Priceless!

Chapter 25
The Widget

What in the world is a Widget? A complete history of Delta and its logo is well known except for how "The Widget" got its name. Nobody seems to know why the logo is called a "Widget". When the little crop-dusting company from Macon, Georgia got into the passenger business it decided to change the company name. They looked for a short name, preferably with five letters. It was a secretary by the name of Miss Fitzgerald, who said, "Delta.'" The new name fits the crop-dusting company, formerly known as Huff Daland Dusters, that was now based in Monroe, Louisiana, and operated throughout the Mississippi Delta region.

The new name influenced the shape of Delta's first passenger service logo—a triangle—representing the "D" of the Greek alphabet, which is "Delta." At center is a winged Mercury, the Roman god of travel and commerce. Early logos also featured the Norse god Thor and the Roman god Mercury. Since that time, Delta has had 19 logos. A "delta-shaped" triangle was incorporated in all of them except the "Flying D" logos from 1945-1959.

The first red, white, and navy-blue triangle emblem was introduced in 1959, when Delta entered the jet era with the introduction of the DC-8. Its shape resembles the swept wing appearance of a jet seen overhead. But when was if first called a "Widget"?

The longest duration of any livery was 30 years, which was introduced in 1967. Photos of the "delta wing" shape of a military jet flying overhead sparked the Delta "Widget". Richard Maurer, Delta senior vice president—general counsel and secretary, noticed the similarity between the Greek delta triangle and the shape of the new jets, and shared his thoughts with Delta's advertising agency Burke Dowling Adams (BDA) in a letter in 1955. Robert Bragg, vice president of Delta's advertising agency, is credited as the designer of the Delta Widget. But, was he the one who first called it a "Widget"?

The Widget evolved from Royal Jet Service emblem into the Delta's corporate logo that was in use for the next fifty years. Delta's advertising department invested values into each of the logo's colors of red, white and blue and its strong triangle shape: The blue portion points to the sky where we fly—the point represents the pinnacle of professional achievement; the swept wing of the jet is represented by the broad white 'V'; the flat broad base suggests Delta's solid foundation. Colored red, it can be regarded not only as the exhaust behind the jet, but also the flame of leadership that keeps the point headed upward.

Delta's logo for half a century got a modern touch in March 2000. The traditional angle of the red triangle base was replaced with a curved line. Delta described the design philosophy behind the new "softer" widget, "Research has told us the logo device is hard and militaristic, not warm, approachable. To retain a link to the past while moving us into the 21st century, we can better align the new version to our current strategy and our efforts to be the passenger's airline. We keep the strength of the mark, but make it warmer, softer, more inviting, thus the curved edges."

The modern 3-dimensional Red Widget was introduced in 2007, after Delta exited from Chapter 11 bankruptcy protection and merged with Northwest Airline. Lippincott Mercer developed Delta's new look. "The brand identity program signals to the world that Delta is eager to regain its leadership position and is committed to improving the customer experience," said Creative Director Connie Birdsall. "Delta's updated look is bold and confident and connects to the customer with honesty, respect and authenticity."

The Delta Brand Council, a cross-divisional team, also contributed to the transformation process, for the first time incorporating the voices of Delta employees into a brand change.

The Merriam-Webster dictionary defines "Watchamacallit" as a word used when the actual name of the object in question will not come to mind. It defines "Thingamajig" as a thing whose name one has forgotten, does not know, or does not wish to mention. Maybe Delta's easily recognizable logo falls into the same category. Everyone knows what it is when they see it, but nobody knows how it got its name.

Chapter 26
Swan Song

My retirement flight was on the L-1011 from Brussels to Atlanta, at the end of May in 1997, with a hand-picked crew that included: First Officer, Charles "Weazal" Lowery, Second Officer, Sonny Ideker and Flight Attendants Vickie Doolittle and Brenda Newman, as the Inflight Service Coordinators. Carol, our son Jeff, his wife Melinda, and grandkids, Katie, and Taylor, went along to help celebrate this important milestone.

Carol had tee shirts made for Taylor and Katie with my picture on the front and the caption "Grandpa's Last Flight". The flight attendants arranged a party at our favorite pub in Brussels and then we all went to dinner together at a great Italian restaurant around the corner from the Royal Windsor Hotel. We had a wonderful time in Brussels celebrating with the crew on my last layover with Delta Air Lines.

As we prepared to leave the hotel the next morning, Carol had tears in her eyes. I said, "Hey, let's not get emotional"! Carol said, "I'm just thinking, this will be the last time we will be able stay in a nice hotel like this for free"! We both had a good chuckle!

The flight attendants had the entire cabin of the airplane decorated with retirement banners, signs, and balloons. As the passengers boarded, they were told that it was Captain Stowe's retirement flight. They were all excited to be a part of the festivities. However, the excitement didn't last. As we turned onto the runway for takeoff, the First Officers flight instruments failed. We weren't going anywhere!

We called ground control and requested permission to return to the gate. Instead, we were directed to a remote section of the tarmac of the airport to wait for a mechanic to come have a look. If we returned to the gate, passengers would have to go through another security screening before re-boarding, so the stations people made the decision to keep us on the tarmac with the passengers on the aircraft.

It took over an hour for the mechanics to get to our airplane. They were busy dispatching the flight to JFK. It was getting hot on the airplane and the passengers were getting irritable. We opened the doors to get some ventilation, but this did not help much. The mechanics finally arrived and found a fuse that powered the instruments had failed. They went to look for a spare fuse, but there were none to be had. Other airlines were called, but nobody had a spare fuse. It was getting hotter and hotter on the airplane and people were beginning to be concerned about missing their connecting flight in Atlanta.

I too was getting concerned. According to regulations, I would be unable to fly after midnight since it was past my retirement date. If the flight should cancel, I would be flying home as a passenger the next day. One of the things a pilot looks forward to on his retirement flight is the "water cannon" salute by the fire department as you taxi toward the gate for the last time. In addition, Carol had planned a retirement party at

Malone's Bar and Grill near the airport in Atlanta. All our friends would be at the airport waiting for me to arrive.

The mechanics finally gave up the search for a spare fuse. They call the maintenance control office in Atlanta and was advised that one of our non-essential hydraulic pumps had the same size fuse as the flight instruments. We could be dispatched without the hydraulic pump. Some four hours after turning off the runway, the fuses were swapped. We were finally ready to start our flight to Atlanta. Everyone gave a big sigh of relief!

After landing in Atlanta, I made a PA announcement and invited my family to the cockpit to witness the "water cannon salute". Weazal puts my grandson Taylor on his lap and asked if he would like to "drive" the airplane to the gate. Five-year-old Taylor shook his head yes. Of course, Taylor didn't know the control wheel is only used in flight – it has no effect while taxiing the aircraft on the ground. I was controlling the aircraft with a nose steering wheel on my left, but Taylor couldn't see this from the copilot's seat. Whenever we got close to a turning point, Weazal would say. "Turn the wheel Taylor". Taylor would move the control wheel in the direction of the turn. As the aircraft begin to respond, Taylor had a big grin on his face. Yes, he really thought he was driving the airplane.

Most of my friends waited around until my flight arrived and then we all headed over to Malone's for a big party.

I thank God for a wonderful career that allowed me to see parts of the world that many people only dream about. And, I think God for allowing me the opportunity to work for Delta Air Lines and meet some of the most wonderful people on Earth, who made my career so rewarding.

Chapter 27
Bringing Her Home

In February of 2019, it was rumored that the Delta Flight Museum was negotiating with International Air Response (IAR) to purchase a DC-7B for display at its facility in Atlanta, Georgia. This was the first airplane I was trained to fly for Delta Air Lines some 53 years ago in 1966.

The aircraft was stored at Coolidge Municipal Airport in Arizona and had done little flying since the early 2000s. The aircraft, registered as N4887C, was delivered to Delta Air Lines in November of 1957, and assigned ship number 717. She was operated by several travel clubs after being retired from the airline in 1968 and then sold to IAR's predecessor T&G Aviation in June 1980. The airplane was converted to a fire bomber and assigned #33. It fought forest fires around the continental U.S. and Alaska until 2000, when it was last based in Palmer, Alaska. In early 2000, it was painted in vintage Delta Airlines colors and, for a short time, also carried Delta Air Lines titles. The airline did not find this amusing. While most of the passenger interior has been removed, the original horseshoe lounge in the rear of the aircraft remains largely intact.

The sale of this iconic 1950s airliner would require one final flight to its home in Atlanta. Two previous attempts to ferry the aircraft from Coolidge Airport to the IAR headquarters at Phoenix-Mesa Gateway Airport resulted in aborted takeoffs and plans to move the aircraft were put on hold. Despite some serious engine problems, the aircraft was in good condition. The necessary repairs would have to be made at the Coolidge Airport.

By April, progress had been made in preparing the aircraft for flight. The fuel system was the primary area of concentration: fixing the numerous small leaks, rehabbing valves, and pumps, and waiting for the tanks to be re-sealed. The company had to buy eight fuel pumps just to get four that would run. Since their removal from other aircraft, the pumps had probably been sitting on a shelf for years. The only way to check their internal seals was to install them into the tanks, then add fuel and see if they leaked. After completing these tasks, the plan was to run the engines and do a taxi test. This was followed by a weight and balance check and swinging the landing gear to make sure it would retract and extend.

A major milestone was achieved in May, when the engines were run without any major problems. All four engines were running with varying results, but nothing serious was discovered. Just a few minor issues that needed to be resolved. The engines were first turned thru by the starters (no fuel or ignition) with the bottom spark plugs removed. This was done to prevent oil that may have settled in the lower cylinders from causing hydraulic lock damage during engine start. Once this was done, the engines were started and run in sequence from #1 to #4. The planned procedure was that once the engines warmed, they were to be brought up to a high-power setting. While at the high power setting the props

two engines were leased from Erickson Aero Tanker. Since the aircraft would be on static display, there was no need for serviceable engines. Both leased engines would be returned to Erickson. The hydraulic leak on the right main landing gear was repaired and high-speed taxi runs were successfully completed.

Welcome Home Old Girl

The ferry flight finally departed the Phoenix-Mesa Gateway Airport on November 16th. She made an overnight fuel stop in Midland, Texas and arrived at ATL shortly after 5:00 pm on Sunday, November 17th. The beautiful lady made a graceful flyover of the airport and circled the field, before making the final landing of her long and distinguished career. A great ending to the almost year-long saga to get this iconic former Delta airliner to the museum in Atlanta. The trip was flown at 9,500 feet in the depressurized aircraft, for a combined 6.5 hours in the air. She headed over to Delta's TechOps facility for restoration.

Detailed information about the work performed on N4887C was reported by Bill Van Dyck on the website, Propliner Info Exchange. The Delta Flight Museum made the official announcement just as N4887C was landing in Atlanta. Ship 717 taxied to Delta TechOps' north hangars, where it will undergo some minor cosmetic repairs before a final painting and installation in front of historic hangars at the Delta Flight Museum.

Chapter 28
The Black Swan

A Black Swan is an unpredictable event that is beyond what is normally expected of a situation and has potentially severe consequences. Black Swan events are characterized by their extreme rarity and their severe impact. As of this writing in March of 2020, the world is experiencing a global pandemic caused by the COVID-19 viral disease that has rapidly swept across the globe, causing major havoc to the world economy.

The airline industry has seen periods of boom and bust since their beginning. During good economic conditions, an airline can be a cash cow, but during the bad periods, they hemorrhage cash at an alarming rate.

Birth of the Airline Industry

After the birth of flight in 1903, flying was a risky endeavor not commonplace until 1925 when the Air Mail Act facilitated the development of the airline industry by allowing the postmaster to contract with private airlines to deliver mail. Shortly thereafter, the Air Commerce Act gave the Secretary of Commerce power to establish airways, certify aircraft, license pilots, and issue and enforce air traffic regulations. Within 10 years, many modern-day airlines, such as United and American, had emerged as major players.

In 1938, the Civil Aeronautics Act established the Civil Aeronautics Board. This board served numerous functions, the two most significant being determining airline routes of travel and regulating prices for passenger fares. The CAB based airfares on average costs. Because airlines couldn't compete by offering lower fares, they competed by striving to offer the best quality service. If the CAB found an airline's service quality was lacking on a certain route, it would allow other carriers to begin operating on that route. In this environment, established airlines enjoyed an advantage over startups, as new carriers found it difficult to break into existing routes. The Federal Aviation Agency, now known as the Federal Aviation Administration (FAA), was created in 1958 to manage safety operations.

Airline Deregulation

In the mid-1970s, Alfred Kahn, an economist and deregulation advocate, became chairman of the CAB. Around the same time, a British airline began offering exceptionally inexpensive transatlantic flights, awakening a desire for US based airlines to lower their fares. These influences led to Congress passing the Airline Deregulation Act of 1978, ushering in an era of unencumbered free market competition. The CAB disbanded a few years thereafter. Post-deregulation, new carriers rushed into the market, and new routes directly connected cities previously accessible only via a string of layovers. Fares dropped as competition and the number of customers increased.

Air Traffic Controllers Strike

On August 3, 1981, over 85 percent of the 17,500 air traffic controllers went on strike for better working conditions and improved wages. The strike brought about a temporary setback to airline growth and profitability as 7,000 flights across the country were canceled. The same day, President Reagan called the strike illegal and threatened to fire any controller who had not returned to work within 48 hours. Two days later, an angry President Reagan carried out his threat, and the federal government began firing the 11,359 air-traffic controllers who had not returned to work. They were initially replaced by controllers, supervisors and staff personnel not participating in the strike and in some cases, by military controllers. Then thousands of people were hired as permanent replacements for the fired controllers.

After President Reagan replaced the controllers and the air traffic control system returned to normal, airline traffic and growth continued for the remainder of the decade. However, some of the major carriers who had dominated the skies during the middle portion of the century, such as Pan American and TWA, began to collapse in the wake of competition. Such carriers disappeared completely following the Gulf War and subsequent recession of the early 1990s. Surviving airlines rode out the recession and returned to record profitability by the late 1990s.

Nine-Eleven

In 2001, the industry dealt with the effects of another economic downturn, as business travel decreased substantially while labor and fuel costs increased. Then, the terrorist attacks of 9/11 shook the United States in a profound way, deeply upsetting the national perception of safety within U.S. borders. No industry or sector of the economy felt the impacts of these events more than the airline industry. Both the immediate reaction to the attacks and the long-term repercussions negatively affected the industry.

On September 11, 2001, a total of 240 flights were rerouted to Canada when American airspace was closed after the terrorist attacks on New York and Washington, and 39 of those flights ended up in Gander, Newfoundland. The townspeople of Gander (and surrounding areas) came through magnificently in the crisis, as 6,579 marooned passengers and crew members swelled their population by two-thirds. A Delta flight attendant and many of the passengers wrote detailed accounts of their experiences that have been widely published. The following is a condensed version of their stories.

Thank God for Gander

A flight attendant remembers: We were about 5 hours out of Frankfurt flying over the North Atlantic and I was in my crew rest seat taking my scheduled break. Suddenly, the curtains parted, and I was told to go to the cockpit to see the captain. As soon as I got there, I noticed the crew had one of those "all business" looks on their faces. The captain handed me a printed message. I quickly read the message and realized the importance of it. The message was from Atlanta, addressed to our flight, and simply said, "All airways over the Continental US are closed. Land ASAP at the nearest airport, advise your destination." Until we knew more, the decision was made to lie to the passengers. They were told that we were diverting into Gander with "instrument problems".

When we landed in Gander there were other airplanes on the ground from all over the world. After we parked on the ramp the captain made the following announcement. "Ladies and gentlemen, you must be wondering if all these airplanes have the same instrument problems that we have. The reality is that we are here for a good reason." Then he went on to explain the little bit we knew about the situation in the US. The time at Gander was 12:30 pm local time.

No one was allowed off the aircraft and no one on the ground could come near except police vehicles. Airways over the North Atlantic were soon vacated, and Gander ended up with airplanes from all over the world, many flying US flags. We were told that airplanes would be offloaded, one at a time, with the foreign carriers given the priority. We were number 14 to be offloaded in the US category. We were further told that we would be given a tentative time to deplane at 6:00 pm. Meanwhile, bits of news started to come in over the aircraft radio and for the first time we learned that airplanes were flown into the World Trade Center in New York and into the Pentagon in Washington. True to their word, at 6:00 pm Gander airport told us that our turn to deplane would come at 11:00 am, the next morning.

The next 23 hours were spent locked on-board the airplane, before being transported to the Salvation

Army in Lewisporte for processing. Gander and the surrounding communities closed all the high schools, meeting halls, lodges, and any other large gathering places. These facilities were converted into mass lodging areas with cots, sleeping bags, and pillows. High school students took care of the passengers in these facilities.

Elderly passengers were taken to private homes. One young pregnant lady was taken to a private home right across the street from a 24-hour Urgent Care type facility. The people of Lewisporte and the Salvation Army fed passengers three meals a day and provided countless blankets, toothbrushes and toiletries by residents and businesses. The elementary school next to the Salvation Army building canceled classes for its children to provide passenger access to the much-needed shower stalls and the computer classroom for them to e-mail home.

The crew was taken to a hotel where they finally found out the total scope of the terror back home by turning on the television.

Two days later, the crew was taken to the airport for a 12:30 pm departure for Atlanta. Back on the aircraft, the passengers had totally bonded, and they were calling each other by their first names, exchanging phone numbers, addresses, and email addresses. One of our passengers asked if he could speak over the PA to his fellow passengers. He reminded everyone about what they had just gone through in the last few days and the hospitality they had received at the hands of total strangers. He said that he would like to do something in return for the good folks of the town of Lewisporte. He suggested setting up a Trust Fund under the name of DELTA 15 (our flight number). The purpose of the trust fund would be to provide a scholarship for high school students of Lewisporte. He asked for donations of any amount from his fellow travelers. The total amount collected was 14,000 dollars. The doctor from Virginia promised to match the donations and to start the administrative work on the scholarship. The fund has since generated about 1.5 million dollars in donations.

Bankruptcy

After 9/11 the airlines continued losing money for years, before finally returning to profitability in 2006. During the interim, most every major carrier in the United States, including Delta, filed for Chapter 11 Bankruptcy Protection. After stripping much of their debt and terminating many of the company sponsored retirement plans in bankruptcy, Delta returned to making a profit. Its revenue increased from $19.1 billion in 2007 to $47.7 billion dollars in 2019 and the airline even paid out $1.6 billion in profit sharing checks to its employees.

COVID – 19

Early in 2020 came the word that a new virus had been diagnosed in Wuhan, China, a city of 11 million people. Airlines worldwide stopped service to China, but the virus had already started spreading around the world and country after country, including the United States, saw thousands of people become infected.

The Black Swan event brought the world to its knees. Delta slashed its capacity by 70% and consolidated facilities at airports around the country. At its Atlanta (ATL) hub, the largest in the world, it "minimized use" of Concourses C, D and E — a move designed to shrink it to roughly its 1980s footprint at the airport. Delta also closed Terminal 3 in Los Angeles (LAX), Terminal 2 at New York John F. Kennedy (JFK), and parts of Terminal D at New York LaGuardia (LGA) amid facility adjustments across its network.

By the middle of March, one of the runways and several taxiways at the Atlanta International Airport were closed to make space for parking Delta airplanes. Just imagine, a two-mile-long runway with airplanes parked wingtip to wingtip. Hundreds of airplanes were flown to the desert storage facility in Victorville, California.

Delta already had plans to retire its McDonnell Douglas MD-88 and MD-90 jets, as well as some Boeing 767s. However, due to the crisis, more fleet changes may come depending on the length and depth of the downturn.

"If Delta survives this, it will emerge as a much smaller airline" CFO Paul Jacobson told employees during an internal webinar on Thursday, March 19th. "The expectation is that the recovery in demand will be slow at first." Delta CEO Ed Bastian said that 17,000 of the carrier's 91,000 active employees had already taken a voluntary unpaid leave package.

A smaller Delta will also mean changes to the airline's route map. Delta maintains core hubs in Atlanta (ATL), Detroit (DTW), Minneapolis/St. Paul (MSP) and Salt Lake City (SLC), plus secondary — or "coastal" — hubs in Boston (BOS), Los Angeles (LAX), New York John F. Kennedy (JFK) and LaGuardia (LGA), and Seattle (SEA). It has focus cities in smaller markets, including Austin (AUS), Cincinnati (CVG), Nashville (BNA) and Raleigh/Durham (RDU). Routes between Delta hubs and those of its partners abroad will likely remain but those to secondary cities — both in the U.S. and abroad — could be cut.

For now, at least, Delta and other airlines are in survival mode, winding down schedules and cutting costs to save cash to bridge them through the duration of the crisis. Already, two U.S. regional carriers — Compass Airlines and Trans States Airlines — have said they will close their doors permanently because of major airlines' reductions. "Our 100% priority and focus right now is making sure we get through the dark parts and see the light of day at the end," Jacobson told employees in the webinar.

Delta was burning $50 million per day. Airline employees were being asked to reduce their hours – and pay — to help cut expenses. Ground staff reduced their workweeks to three or four days, a move designed to reduce payroll by as much as a quarter over 90 days.

In late March, the Congress passed a $2 trillion emergency relief bill aimed at limiting the financial trauma that the coronavirus pandemic is inflicting on the United States. The airline industry, which has suffered huge losses because of canceled flights and travel restrictions, would be a top recipient in the bill. Passenger airlines would qualify for $50 billion in loans and certain other guarantees. Delta CEO Ed Bastian said, "Delta expects to receive between $5 billion and $10 billion from the package that would be exclusively used for the continuation of payment of employee wages, salaries, and benefits."

Considering the unprecedented challenges facing the company, Delta has entered into a $2.6 billion secured credit agreement and is drawing down $3 billion under its existing revolving credit agreements. In the meantime, Delta employees are pulling together in the spirit that has always pulled Delta through rough times.

By the first week in April, Delta had shut down its international operation. Prior to COVID-19 Delta operated hundreds of international flights from the United States to 41 destinations in Europe, but many countries in Europe are under shelter-in-place orders by their governments. After April 7th, the only international service to Europe was one daily flight from Atlanta (ATL) to Amsterdam (AMS) and one flight, 4 days a week, from Detroit (DTW) to Amsterdam.

By May, the decision was made to permanently remove the entire fleet of B-777s from the schedule. This had been Delta's long-haul aircraft and a major part of the international operation. The system-wide load factor was only 30 percent, with a breakeven load factor of 80 percent. The airline was still losing 50 million dollars per day.

Delta estimated that it will be over staffed by 7,000 pilots in the fall of 2020. If the pandemic subsides, the recovery of passenger traffic is expected to be slow. The company still expects to be over staffed by 3500 pilots in the 2nd quarter of 2021. Major layoffs appear to be on the horizon.

In mid-June, states begin to lift restrictions and Delta begin to add flights, but with limited capacity. Flights were only booked at 60% capacity with all center seats left vacant for social distancing. This was done to make people more comfortable with flying in crowded aircraft. Delta announced that it would add 1000 daily flight by August and re-evaluate the situation after Labor Day.

Then in July came the word that many states were starting to experience record numbers of people being tested positive for the virus, as businesses started to reopen. The virus was once again raging out of control in many parts of the country. Delta announced that it was going to scale back its expansion plans in August. Seventeen thousand Delta employees accepted an early retirement offer that would help to reduce the number of people that might be facing a furlough in the fall.

Time will tell if guidelines designed to contain the virus are being followed and if Delta is able to survive the worst economic situation in its history.

Founded as Huff-Daland Dusters on May 2, 1925, Delta is the oldest continually operating airline company in the United States.

Historical Information about the Black Swan events was gathered from the Newspaper.com website. Information about how Delta is dealing with COVID-19 was published in the Atlanta Constitution newspaper and other printed sources quoting Delta officials.

Eastern Airlines, Flight Attendant Class
February 1962

Delta Air Lines, Pilot Class
March 1966

Delta Air Lines, Retirement
May 1997

Grandpa's Last Flight

DL 125, Brussels to Atlanta
May 31, 1997

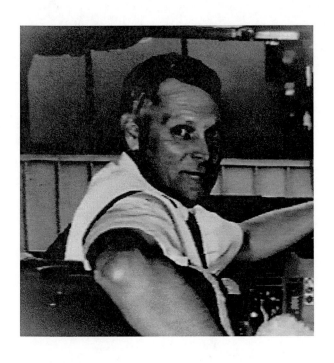

"Travel is fatal to prejudice, bigotry, and narrow-mindedness, and many of our people need it sorely on these accounts. Broad, wholesome, charitable views of men and things cannot be acquired by vegetating in one little corner of the earth all one's lifetime."

...........Mark Twain